SAM CAMPBELL

Philosopher of the Forest

by Shandelle Marie Henson

*There is a source of wonderment,
greater than stellar magnitudes,
the tricks of time,
or the miracle of growth.
It is that we are here
and have within us the ability
to know beauty, to be kind,
to experience patience, peace,
and deep piety.*

—Nature's Messages

TEACH Services, Inc.
New York

PRINTED IN THE UNITED STATES OF AMERICA
World rights reserved. This book or any portion thereof may not be copied or reproduced in any form or manner whatever, except as provided by law, without the written permission of the publisher, except by a reviewer who may quote brief passages in a review.

2005 06 07 08 09 10 11 12 · 5 4 3 2 1

The author assumes full responsibility for the accuracy of all facts and quotations as cited in this book.

Copyright © 2001 Three Lakes Historical Society
Three Lakes, Wisconsin

Copyright © 2002 TEACH Services, Inc.
ISBN 1-57258-221-9
Library of Congress Catalog Card No. 2001094238

Published by

TEACH Services, Inc.
www.TEACHServices.com

Samuel Arthur Campbell
1895–1962

This book is dedicated to

Audrey and John Henson,
my dear mom and dad,
who have always encouraged my dreams.

Table of Contents

Part One... THE BEGINNINGS
1895–1928

1. Voices of the Woods! 3
2. Wegimind, My Mother 10
3. Bind Up the Broken-hearted 19
4. Scars of Our Folly 29
5. Think on These Things 35
6. Land of the Voyaguers! 46
7. Spirit of the Wilderness 60
8. Giny 67

Part Two... LIFE AT ITS BEST
1929–1962

9. Sanctuary of Wegimind 75
10. Just a Beginning 81
Afterword   Jean Cunningham Brewster 85

Sources and other information by chapter

Appendix One 86
Appendix Two 89
Appendix Three 92
Appendix Four 93
Appendix Five 95
Appendix Six 97
Appendix Seven 99
Appendix Eight 101
Appendix Nine 103
Appendix Ten 105

Miscellany

Notes on Sam Campbell's Surviving Family 111
Bibliography 160

Acknowledgements

I wrote this book over a period of several years while in graduate school. There were times when I doubted it would ever be completed. I wish to thank all of those whose help and encouragment motivated me to finish this manuscript.

When I first decided to research the life of Sam Campbell, I called the home of his friend Sigurd Olson in Ely, Minnesota. I didn't realize Mr. Olson had recently passed away, but his wife Elizabeth Olson graciously answered my questions and suggested I call Walter Goldsworthy of Three Lakes, Wisconsin.

When I contacted Walt Goldsworthy, I realized I had hit the jackpot of Sam Campbell information and enthusiasm! John "Walt" Goldsworthy is administrator of the Three Lakes Museum and one of the founders of the Three Lakes Historical Society. He is also a writer, philosopher, environmentalist, and former forest service naturalist. In the tradition of Sam Campbell, he has been a wise mentor for many young people, and is the prime motivator behind most of the major community projects launched in the Three Lakes area. "Uncle Walt" was a friend of Sam Campbell's during Sam's later years. He, along with Jean Brewster, have contributed the bulk of the information in this book. Without Uncle Walt, I would have never started this book, and certainly would have never finished it!

Walt Goldsworthy introduced me to Jean Cunningham Brewster of Three Lakes. Jean grew up around Sam Campbell, who had been "adopted" by the Cunninghams as part of the family. Jean and her sister Beth appeared in Sam's books as the composite character "June." Sam always described June as a beautiful, dark-haired, athletic girl. I first met Jean Brewster when

Michael J. Battistone and I attended the dedication of the Sam Campbell Memorial Trail Complex in Three Lakes on June 29, 1989. I immediately knew who she was without even being introduced. She is a dark-eyed, beautiful, energetic lady—just the way I had pictured a grown-up June. She warmly and graciously answered our questions, and has added a host of details from her tremendous memory.

I also wish to thank Doris Goldsworthy for her help with historical details, her excellent proof reading, and her hospitality. Norman Brewster also helped with historical details and contributed anecdotes. Doris and Walt Goldsworthy, and Jean and Norm Brewster read the manuscript, as did my parents John and Audrey Henson, and my friend David Banks.

Michael J. Battistone helped with the initial research and wrote part of Chapter One (see Appendix One). He generated a lot of the early enthusiasm for the project.

Further thanks are due to the Three Lakes Historical Society, The Watseka Historical Society, Evelyn Frandsen, Robert Gentry, Norman Hallock, Jan Haluska, Judy Hanson, Henry Haskell, H. Lyle Hinz, Dorothy Hoelter, Doug Jordan, Diedre Kieckhefer, Robert M. Kieckhefer, Doris and George Koller, Betty Lamon, Ralph Leatzow, Art Meyers, Violet Olkowski, Elizabeth Olson, Sigurd T. Olson, Jr., Jim Pascoe, Gertrude Puelicher, John Sanstead, Janet Wolfe, and Ruth Yeager; also to Julie du Mars and Constance Wilson, archivists at The First Church of Christ, Scientist in Boston, and to many others.

The photographs are courtesy of Jean Brewster and the Three Lakes Museum. The origin of a few of the photographs is unknown; I regret any cases in which I have been unable to give proper credit.

I have endeavored to blend the sometimes conflicting written records and oral accounts into a factual life story. I regret any errors.

Introduction

My parents were students at Collegedale Academy and Southern Missionary College in Collegedale, Tennessee during the late 1940's and early 1950's. Like many young people of the day, they became acquainted with Sam Campbell through their school's lyceum programs. Sam Campbell was a favorite on the lecture circuit all over the country. He would come to speak on conservation and narrate his interesting and often hilarious movies of north woods animal life.

My parents bought our family's first Sam Campbell books in 1969. They were the green hardcover first editions published by Bobbs-Merrill Company. I was too young to enjoy the books, and they sat on our bookshelves by the fireplace, patiently waiting.

When I was a few years older, WSMC–FM, the local radio station, hosted a children's program every Sunday night called "Just For Kids." Joyce Dick, who was later my high school English teacher, did an excellent job reading children's books for this program. Her renditions of Sam Campbell's stories especially stirred my imagination, and before long I discovered the exciting green books by the fireplace.

At first I read the books for their story content, and skipped over the descriptive prose and philosophy. I loved the books so much, however, that I read them over and over, each time reading more of the "boring" parts. These passages had a profound influence on my young mind. By the time I reached the seventh grade, I had become sensitive to the beauty of nature, I had a deep interest in philosophy and spiritual matters, and I was already a conservationist.

I also had a severe case of wanderlust. Sam wrote in one of his books that as a youngster, he sometimes became literally ill with his desire for wilderness. I knew exactly what he meant! I longed for backpacking and canoeing trips; I dreamed of far-off places like Lake Louise, the Grand Canyon, and Canadian canoe country. I fretted to see panthers, moose, beaver, and river otters in the wild. Sometimes as a child, I too felt quite ill with these longings.

A childhood friend named Greg Phillips was also a big Sam Campbell fan. He and I used to quote long passages of the books by memory, and interminably go through that crazy "Squoip" routine from *A Tippy Canoe and Canada Too*. We ordered maps from Minnesota's Boundary Waters Canoe Area Wilderness and pored over them for hours, retracing Sam Campbell's routes through the maze of lakes. We were determined to locate the mysterious "Sanctuary Lake" and go there someday. Greg and I carefully planned many canoe trips to the area, but we were too young to do more than dream.

As a young adult, I suddenly realized I was at last in a position to begin indulging my dreams of wilderness. Since then, I have spent nearly every spare moment backpacking or hiking. I was finally able to make those long-anticipated canoe trips into Boundary Waters!

In June of 1989, I camped for a week with two friends on the north shore of Four Mile Lake near Three Lakes, Wisconsin. This campsite, now in Nicolet National Forest, at one time lay in Campbell's Sanctuary of Wegimind. We could see Sam Campbell's island from our camp! We met many friends of the Campbells', and visited all the special places familiar to Campbell readers such as Vanishing Lake, Four Mile Creek, and Franklin Lake. Two years later, I returned to Three

Lakes to do some more research. Incidentally, throughout all the excitement of these trips, one general impression has remained in my mind. I had been warned not to be disappointed when the places described in Sam Campbell's books turned out to be different from the way I imagined them. The startling thing is that the places look very much like what I have imagined for all these years!

Sam Campbell, naturalist, lecturer, photographer, author and philosopher, was one of the early pioneers in the environmental movement. Campbell's unique approach to conservation was two-fold. First, it was grounded in a philosophy of absolute values. I'll say more about this in a moment. Second, his efforts were aimed at educating and entertaining people (especially children) in hopes of raising their consciousness. Sam Campbell respected the emerging breed of politically active conservationists, and acknowledged a great need for them. However, he found that his own personality was much better suited to low-key, friendly efforts to help people appreciate nature and thus lift their thoughts to more lofty values.

A secular reader may be surprised by the spiritual themes in this story. To understand Sam Campbell, it is essential to recognize that his whole life, including his dedication to conservation, was consistently based on the absolutes of his beliefs about God. Today it is no longer fashionable for forward-thinking people to put their arguments on spiritual foundations. Environmentalists have strong feelings about the morality of protecting the earth, but our arguments are often reduced to pragmatism and utilitarianism. In this account of Campbell's life, I have tried to be faithful to his philosophy as I understand it.

Sam Campbell wrote twelve story books which are now being reprinted by TEACH Services Inc. of Brushton NY. Lesser known are his first book *The Conquest of Grief* and his collection of essays *Nature's Messages*. He also wrote many freelance articles and essays, some of which have been compiled in various sources.

This is the story of Sam Campbell's life, not a comprehensive biography. There is, however, an appendix for each chapter. These appendices (1) separate the chapter's facts from speculation or mere fictional story devices; (2) acknowledge the sources and references for the chapter; and (3) give additional information of interest. I welcome any corrections, comments, and information from readers. Please send correspondence to the publishers.

I have not attempted to detail those years of Sam Campbell's life which are well known to his readers through the twelve story books. Instead, I have concentrated on his early life and on those forces which formed him into the well-loved character known to millions as "The Philosopher of the Forest."

Sam Campbell died unexpectedly in 1962, two years before I was born. He influenced my life only through his books. A set of twelve story books may seem a small thing, but it is impossible to overestimate the influence Sam Campbell had on my life. He taught me to value faith, the Still Small Voice, solitude, wilderness, and friendship. I have met hundreds of others, from grade school children to the very elderly, who have been similarly enriched. How we thank God for the humble, joyful, hilarious naturalist, his pet animals, and his wonderful books!
—*Shandelle Marie Henson*

Foreword

Sam Campbell, the "Philosopher of the Forest," was a legend of the North Country. Once met, he was never forgotten, for he was a fountain of inspiration and buoyant enthusiasm. He enriched and inspired man's appreciation for the power and glory of God manifested in all of creation.

I first met Sam some 40 years ago in 1948. I have never forgotten the moment.

It was an evening in early December. The Three Lakes Rotary Club was gathered to present him with a new toboggan to haul supplies from the mainland to his island home.

Snowflakes drifted in behind him as he entered the lighted hall where he was to be special guest of the evening dinner. A red Hudson Bay jacket and a fur cap accented his ruddy face wreathed in smiles of happiness as he greeted old friends.

I was a new comer. We had never met. He took my hand, and the firmness of his grip assured me here indeed was a fellow lover of the great outdoors. There was an aura of almost mystical charm about Sam, an inspiring, joyful nature that captivated his listeners as he shared their companionship.

Over the years, as our acquaintanceship grew and developed into deeper friendship, many new avenues into the realm of nature opened up to me. Heretofore my value of nature had been more utilitarian—that of the hunter and trapper. I was a challenger of the natural law and oftentimes the civil law that attempted to favor the creatures of the forest.

Sam taught me compassion for the lesser creatures of creation. He led me to realize that the forest was, as Bryant has said, "God's ancient sanctuaries;" and that in the halls of these verdant temples, the soul of man is refreshed, and a thinking man is filled with wonderment.

Because of Sam, I came to be conscious of the depths of creation, for Sam once wrote, "What more fitting place to worship than the forest where there is such multiform evidence of Him whose name is Love!" I came to learn that here in the depths of these ancient cathedrals, all life moves to laws not of its own, but to those which attest to the infinite power and intelligence of the Creator of all.

Sam fostered within me a richer appreciation for the fog-filled sunrises along these northern waterways, the haunting cries of loons, the glow of a campfire, the calls of owls, music of the coyotes, the splash of beaver in the nighttime waters. Each took on a mantle of spiritual refreshment as the years unfolded. From Sam I learned of the stellar constellation Capella, "Queen of the North." Sam called her the guardian of the wilderness nights, for Capella never sets, but circles the northern skies. My moments as a sojourner in far places are always brightened when I seek out the friendly glitter of this Queen.

The doors of wilderness joy and wisdom which Sam opened for me, he opened for millions of others who were exposed to his films, lectures and books.

Now, as I have lived my three score and ten years and have embarked on the four score mark of time, I can only hope and pray that all those who come to walk the Sam Campbell Trail Complex which winds through the timbered highlands north of Four Mile Lake, the locale of Sam's Island home Wegimind, will catch that golden spirit of Sam's philosophy as they explore the shadowy avenues of the virgin forest and catch the enchantment of Vanishing Lake, that jewel of Sam Campbell Country.

Thank you, Sam Campbell!

Walt Goldsworthy
Three Lakes, Wisconsin

Prologue

It was late in the summer of 1929.

A lone birchbark canoe moved silently along the north shore of Four Mile Lake in the early morning light. A family of loons watched from the protective shadows of a small island a few hundred yards away. Occasionally one of the parent birds would lift its head and call out its haunting wail.

To the loons, the canoe appeared to be a log floating along the far bank, partially obscured by the mists rising from the warm water into the chilly morning air. The electric blue chamois shirt worn by the man who guided the craft seemed to the loons a piece of the sky come down to get a morning drink from the lake. They did not see the silent j-strokes, nor the little whirling vortices left behind by the broad blade of his paddle in the silky water.

The man's heavy khaki britches were tucked into high moccasin boots laced up to his knees. His prematurely graying, thinning brown hair ruffled in the slight breeze caused by the forward motion of the canoe. The movements of his powerful arms and broad chest were fluid and unhurried; he and his bark craft formed a perfectly natural part of the wild surroundings.

Sam felt the peace of the morning fill his soul. He nudged the bow of his canoe onto a short sandy beach, and lay back in the gently rocking craft, his face turned up towards the deepening blue of the morning sky. His eyes closed.

Part One

THE BEGINNINGS

1895–1928

SAM CAMPBELL Philosopher Of The Forest

Chapter One

Voices of the Woods!

> *Those who dwell in the woods know these voices well, and they love them as part of the mysterious beauty of the wilderness. But one must be a good listener to hear them. We do not catch these voices if our thoughts are in a whirlwind of our own making.*
> —*Too Much Salt and Pepper*

He loved rivers. Maybe it was because of the songs they sang on their way to the sea, or perhaps he was intrigued by the mystery of something which in one sense was always changing, and in another, timeless. Or maybe he was simply a boy in search of adventure, and like Huck Finn, he knew where this elusive prey would most likely be found. For whatever reason, young Sam Campbell chose to make his first camp on the banks of the Iroquois River in northeastern Illinois. It was the "first date" in a love affair which was to inspire him throughout his life.

Samuel Arthur Campbell was no newcomer to this country. He had been born here in Watseka on August 1, 1895. Four years later, his parents had moved to Chicago, but every summer they returned for a vacation on his grandfather's farm. These annual trips were the highlight of the year. It gave his father, Arthur James Campbell, a rest from his job at the Sloan Valve Company, and his mother, Katherine, a chance to visit with her parents.

In fact, everyone liked to visit with Sam's maternal grandparents. Andrew Jackson Lyman, or "Uncle Jack" as he was known in the community, and his wife Elmira

Brandenburg Lyman, were true "old timers." Andrew was the son of John Lyman, Jr., the "first white man to set up residence on the west bank of the Iroquois." Grandfather's storybook seemed endless; he could tell about the trips he used to take to Chicago to sell wheat and corn—in those days, it took a full week and a good team of oxen! Or there were all those stories from the Civil War, during which he nearly died of pneumonia. But the tales he was most frequently called upon to recount were those of the "early days," rich with Indian lore, encounters with wild animals, and all the mystery of those times.

Sam also loved the farm for the "spirit of it." With one hundred, twenty acres of woods, fields and rivers to explore, and a dog named Sport for companionship, these summer visits to the farm held more attraction than Christmas!

And the animals! Of all the aspects of nature, none captivated Sam more than these "forest friends of fur and feather." He was not content with merely observing these creatures; he yearned for relationships with them. His mother tells of an early experience in which Sam approached a flock of Canadian geese. His tiny hand outstretched in a cherub's gesture of friendship, he begged the huge birds to light on his fingers, and "when they didn't do so, he bawled loud and long."

With his mind fixed on the prospects for such high adventure, Sam often found it difficult to concentrate on his performance at school. He would later describe himself as a "poor student in the classroom, always skimming by, never flunking, but coming close to it." Frequently he would lose himself in daydreams of the farm and of wilderness yet unexplored, and never even hear the teacher call his name.

Sam's mother could see that her boy was very bright, but that his young head was too obsessed with nature and woodlore to take much interest in his homework. She would have been worried except for the fact that Sam read voraciously and showed a definite talent for writing and playing musical instruments.

So, she continued to encourage his thirst for knowledge of nature by taking him on long walks to identify trees and flowers, and by spending long hours reading to him of the adventures of the colorful French-Canadian traders, the voyageurs, those carefree men who paddled their birchbark bateaux along the rapids of northern rivers.

This spring, it was particularly difficult for Sam to concentrate. Of all the vacations to his grandfather's farm, he knew this one would be the most exciting yet. He was going on his first camping trip! Of course, he had been camping many times since infancy with his parents, who loved the outdoors, but this would be his first camping trip with just his friends and no adults along to slow things down.

As the day of departure from the city drew near, Sam's anticipation grew. His thoughts were so far away as he sat at his school desk and stared out the window that his poor teacher finally gave up calling on him at all. She was probably almost as happy as he when the long awaited day came.

It was the last day of school. A soft, warm spring breeze sighed through the schoolroom windows and fluttered Sam's brown hair. He had prevailed upon his mother that morning to let him wear his "woods clothes," a red wool shirt with tough khaki britches and little lumberjack boots with heavy wool socks.

The teacher finally made her obligatory goodbye speech and had them stand for prayer. Sam heard nothing until the final words, "You may go, now." Oh, the delicious sense of freedom! School was out, and he was on his way to Grandfather's farm and a very special camping trip!

The bright yellow flames of the campfire receded slowly, transforming the old, dark logs into orange embers and finally, dusky red coals. The entire display was quite similar to the brilliant sunset only a few hours before. Sam had been observing this process so intently that he failed to notice his companions turning in one by one as the stars came out. He was alone by the fire.

As he lay there on his sleeping roll, looking in vain for a glimpse of the Northern Lights, he was startled by the sound of human voices! As near as he could tell, they appeared to be coming from a point just beyond the bend of the river. Although he could not discern how many there were, they seemed to be in a pleasant mood, and Sam judged them to be fellow campers who had arrived too late to set up camp during daylight.

Lighting a lantern, he waved it in circles, hoping to attract the attention of the party, but without success. He stopped again to listen, but was greeted only with silence. The voices had vanished!

Puzzled, he returned to camp and got ready for bed. He closed his eyes, listening to the symphony of the forest. The night was filled with the songs of crickets, tree toads, and the soothing rush of the river.

Suddenly, Sam heard the voices again! Fascinated, he relit the lantern, and walked slowly to the river bank. It was tough going; the thick brush resisted every step, and the absence of the moon heightened the challenge. He eventually reached the bank, and waved the lantern as before. No response. Again, he signaled. Silence.

Slowly, Sam made his way back to camp. He crept back under his blanket and lay there in the darkness, his mind wrestling with possibilities. The most likely culprit was, of course, an animal. Earlier in the day, the boys had noticed fresh tracks made by several deer and what appeared to be a very large fox or coyote. They had selected their campsite near these "animal runways" in hopes of catching a glimpse of these creatures. Could it be that the brilliant flames of the campfire had kept these forest residents at bay until now? Maybe at this very moment a magnificent stag stood along the river bank, pausing for a moment from nocturnal adventures to quench his thirst from the slow moving waters of the Iroquois!

But no; the sounds Sam had heard were not those which he recognized as animal noises. They had a distinctly human quality about them—they were voices! His imagination raced through the stories his grandfather had told. There were tales of pioneers, his own family in fact, who had braved the unknown and uncharted wilderness in the hope of a better life; of the voyageurs, who had paddled and sung their way down this very river not long before.

But by far the most exciting possibility: Indians! In earlier times, this region had been well populated with these people; they were a true nation whose citizens were as much a part of the forest as the animals who also lived there. Those days had since passed, but many old timers in Watseka believed that in some of the more remote areas, small bands of Indians still survived, living off the land as their ancestors had done for centuries.

Could these legends be true, Sam wondered? Was it possible that somewhere else in the forest that night there had been another campfire, one surrounded by chiefs, braves, and Indian princesses? Sam's mind played idly with this romantic notion as his thoughts drifted like so many downy feathers toward sleep.

Suddenly, a twig snapped! The forest, which had been filled with the songs of the night now seemed strangely silent. Sam lay there in the dark, more curious than afraid. He could make out the sounds of breaking brush. The noises were coming from deep within the forest on the other side of the fire pit and were growing steadily closer. Something was moving into the camp!

After what seemed an eternity, the bushes parted, revealing a tall dark figure, clad in deerskin. Sam sat up in astonishment! The Indian raised his hand, and with an explosive, "How!," disappeared.

The boy awoke with a start, and found himself curled in his blanket beside the cold ashes of the firering as the eastern sky slowly began to brighten with the earliest rays of the sun.

He was lying there comfortably, thinking about the previous night, when he suddenly realized he felt somehow different this morning. He recognized a feeling of deep kinship and satisfying companionship with the wilderness, and he somehow knew that this and other wild places held a special meaning for him.

The sounds Sam heard that night along the banks of the Iroquois remained a mystery to the young boy. Later, as a naturalist, he wrote: "The Voices of the Woods...are simply the sounds of the woods...perhaps a little stream singing over rocks...They are the rustle of leaves, the rubbing of two trees together, the moaning of wind through barren boughs. And when we hear these sounds, in our thoughts we liken them to something in our experience. Thus we think they are voices...Those who dwell in the woods know these voices well, and they love them as part of the mysterious beauty of the wilderness. But one must be a good listener to hear them. We do not catch these voices if our thoughts are in a whirlwind of our own making."

Sam heard these voices several more times as a youngster, and he became obsessed for a time with knowing their origin. Eventually, however, as his teen years progressed and he spent most of his time in the forest hunting and trapping with his young friends, the memory of the strange voices faded into a curious childhood fantasy.

Little did he then know how those wilderness voices were to help shape his life and philosophy.

Chapter Two

Wegimind, My Mother

"Our dominion over the world is the dominion of Love—not brutality!"
—*Wegimind, quoted in*
The Conquest of Grief

Katherine "Kittie" Campbell dozed in the shade of an ancient White Pine, her back against its enormous trunk. Bees buzzed in and out of nearby flowers. A family of ducks splashed and dove near the shore of the sky blue waters of Four Mile Lake. A gentle breeze strummed the tops of the trees. The tranquility and laziness of the northwoods summer flowed through her being in a healing flood, soothing away the cares of the city far away. Her pulse slowed; the unnatural race of Chicago life ebbed in her veins as her heart adopted the measured rhythm of the vast forest around her.

Sam and his brother had been the first to introduce this region of northern Wisconsin to the family. They had visited in the summer of 1909, when Sam was 14 years old. Their Uncle Bill Sloan of Chicago, who knew the area, had taken the boys by train to the northwoods for a camping trip. Sam later wrote that he felt he had "someway slipped into Heaven. The far-flung forests, the myriad lakes, the rushing streams and particularly the animal life, all added up to a dream come true."

Sam and his brother Don soon had to return to school in the city, but for many months they talked almost constantly about their wondrous adventures in the northwoods! Their electric enthusiasm for that far off paradise crackled and sparked daily through the

Wegimind, My Mother

classrooms and halls of school, and in the Campbell home. In order to keep the peace, their parents had to make many vague promises that, yes, maybe they could go up there "some day."

Actually, Sam's parents were interested in going to the northwoods for a camping trip. Kittie and her husband Arthur, whom everyone called "Dad," were great nature enthusiasts. They loved to camp, hike, fish and canoe, and taught their children to enjoy these sports. Kittie, especially, loved the wilderness and seemed to actually be a part of it. It was because of this affinity that young Sam began calling her Wegimind, the Ojibway Indian word for "mother."

When Sam's Grandfather Lyman died in March of 1912, the Campbell family, often accompanied by the Sloans, began spending their summers camping in this area of northern Wisconsin, near the logging settlement called Three Lakes.

Their favorite camping spot was on the remote shores of a medium sized, clear lake known as Four Mile Lake. The Campbells with their three children Don, Sam, and Lucille would ride the train from Chicago on the Chicago and Northwestern Railway each summer to Three Lakes. After buying supplies in town and greeting old friends, they would have someone drive them as far as the roads permitted towards their camp site. At the roads' end, a mile or so of water still separated them from their camp in the stand of virgin timber on the east shore of Four Mile Lake. They would traverse this exciting last leg of their journey by rowboat.

Sam was by now in his late teens, a rather bowlegged, stocky youth of great strength. Although he stood only about 5' 4" tall, no one thought of him as short because he had a charisma about him of capability and gentle strength. His brown hair framed a rugged, square-jawed face, with thick dark brows that accented a pair of remarkably bright blue-gray eyes. His mouth was usually set in a big friendly smile which revealed a row of perfect white teeth.

Kittie opened her eyes at the sound of youthful laughter coming from the direction of camp. She smiled to herself as she recognized Sam's enthusiastic voice. She was glad to see him so relaxed and happy. Sometimes, during the long city winters, she grew worried about her younger son. He would sit for hours and read philosophy, poetry, and tales of untamed wilderness. Don loved the outdoors, too, but he was a practical, thoroughly conventional boy. Sam, on the other hand, brooded so much over these books about unspoiled wild places that he sometimes became physically ill with his intense longing to go there. Of course, Kittie loved Don dearly, but she understood her son Sam; they were so very much alike. Perhaps this knowledge was what worried Kittie most of all.

As Kittie approached the canvas tent and the stone fireplace, she heard Sam telling Don, "Ha, you should have seen it! James and I tracked that deer for two miles before I suddenly caught sight of him feeding in a small clearing! I was sighting down the barrel, when all of the sudden there was this snorting sound off to one side in the trees, and the buck jerked up his head to run! I held my breath and squeezed the trigger. Of course, all of this happened almost at once! Anyway, I couldn't believe it, the buck fell! I've never seen such a..." As Sam saw his mother his voice trailed away into a guilty silence.

Sam felt a stab of intense pain at the sad expression which passed involuntarily over his mother's face. He knew how she felt about hunting and trapping, about killing anything. It hurt Kittie Campbell deeply to see any creature in pain. The rest of her family didn't quite understand this extreme twist to sweet Wegimind's personality. Her father had been a hunter and trapper as well as a farmer, and her husband and boys hunted for sport. Sam had thought nothing of joining his pal James, a boy from the village, in a hunting expedition.

Kittie had always tried to keep her opinions on the subject from being abrasive to others, for she realized that to most people of her time, killing animals for food and sport was simply a way of life, part of normal culture. She recognized in Sam, however, the deep tenderness and sensitivity of her own personality. She wondered how he would eventually deal with these traits.

Don surveyed the tension in the air, and conveniently headed down to the lake to scoop up a pail of fresh drinking water. When they were alone, Sam looked at his mother but said nothing. They were unusually close, always sharing every joy and disappointment with each other, laughing together, simply enjoying each other's company; but now Sam stood silent.

Kittie smiled understandingly at her downcast son, put her slender arm around his waist, and hugged him close. "Oh, Sam, it's ok. Go ahead and have your boyish fun out in the woods hunting. Have a good time. There may come a day when you will no longer wish to hunt, but you shouldn't stop just because I don't care for the sport myself. It takes a lot of time and maturity to know oneself, Sam."

She looked into the eyes of her son, her normally teasing, joyous demeanor suddenly serious. "And Sam, when you finally come to know your own unique philosophy of life, then conduct your life as though you were the model after which all mankind is sculptured."

She smiled again and gave him a little push. "Now, quit lollygaggin', and go get some wood for tonight's cooking fire. We're having good old beans, so they'll need to cook for a while. And how about playing your guitar after supper so we can sing around the campfire?"

Sam smiled back gratefully, and turned with a lighter heart to the forest to look for downed wood.

The cold wind howled in off Lake Michigan with a bone-piercing cold. The sky hung heavy with dark gray clouds. Tiny snowflakes, driven before the blast, whirled with the dust and bits of trash down the dirty city streets.

Sam sat at his writing desk, worriedly watching his mother as she stood, pensively looking out the window at the dreary Chicago afternoon. Was it his imagination, or had Mom seemed tired and thin lately? Was she doing too much for others? Almost every day, some poor soul needing food, advice, or solace would come to her door. She never turned them away without help.

That's all, she is just tired, Sam told himself. I'll try to help her more, do more of the housework. Surely when spring comes and we go north, the woods will revive her.

Dad and Don worked long hours every day at Chicago's Sloan Valve Company, which was owned and managed by Sam's "Uncle Bill," William Sloan. Sam had taught guitar, banjo, and mandolin lessons from his own studio on Michigan Avenue, and for a time had sold industrial real estate. Lately, he had stayed home much of the time with his mother and worked on his writing.

Sam's last years of high school had been difficult. He wasn't interested in business, or law, or trades, or any of the careers his friends had decided to pursue. When he imagined himself cooped up day after day in some dark, dingy office or plant, his whole being rebelled; he became sick to his stomach, and sometimes actually ill. He attended Northwestern University and the University of Chicago for a while. He tried selling real estate, and even taught music. It was rewarding and a great deal of fun, but wasn't satisfying. He wanted to be outdoors, devoting all of his time and talent to nature study.

Teachers and friends tried time and again to advise Sam that life is composed mostly of unpleasant work, not relaxing romps in the woods. He felt trapped; he knew intuitively that giving in to these practical demands would somehow pronounce a death sentence on his soul.

Sam considered going back to Watseka to be a farmer like his grandfather, and his grandfather's grandfather. That would be better; at least he could be outside most of the time. But it wasn't really what he wanted. The flat midwestern farmland simply did not convey the mystery of the forests of the north.

Of course, he could be really adventurous and go out west, or to the Yukon to look for gold. But no, that was not what he wanted. It was appealing to think about, but Sam knew he could never be so far from his beloved family.

The one option Sam could imagine was to become a writer. He could go on wilderness outings and then write about them. What a perfect life! And so, Sam had begun to write up the adventures he had during his summers in the north woods. Several of his articles were published in various outdoor magazines, and although Sam was proud and delighted, he was beginning to really worry about the future. He was in his twenties, without a real career, and still living at home. He simply wasn't making nearly enough money to live on his own, and he was becoming embarrassed about letting Don and Dad help support him.

"Mom." Sam pushed his chair back and rose to his feet. "Please go lie down and rest. I'll finish dusting the furniture."

"I'm OK," Kittie assured him. "I was just thinking about poor Mrs. Helfrich down the street. Her husband just passed away, you know, and now she has to run the store as well as raise those two girls alone." The sympathetic pain in her eyes turned suddenly to a mischievous gleam as she regarded Sam. "By the way, Sam, I told her you'd be calling on her daughter Sarah. She's a nice girl, very domestic and delicate. It would be lovely if you married her, because your great-grandfather's wife's name was Sarah, too..."

Kittie began to laugh uproariously as she saw the frustration flood Sam's handsome young face. "Mother," he sputtered, "You know I'm not interested in getting married! Sarah is a nice girl, I remember her from grammar school, but she would want to be in the house all the time! She wouldn't go canoeing or hiking; she'd say it was unladylike! I..." He paused as he realized his mother was teasing, and laughed sheepishly. "Mother!"

At this moment the door slammed shut behind Dad and Don as they came in from work. Dad was singing at the top of his lungs and Don was grinning as he beat time on his leg to the music. Kittie's face lit up at the sight of her husband and older son, and she began at once to spread supper on the round oak table.

Disengaging himself momentarily from the happy chatter around the supper table, Sam glanced at Wegimind. She was laughing and talking animatedly. Perhaps she wasn't paler than usual. Surely she was all right. Oh, of course she was! With renewed assurance in his heart, Sam joined in the discussion with enthusiasm; and the happy family sat there in the unbroken circle, talking and joking until long after the food had disappeared.

The golden rays of the early morning sun slanted through the sitting room window in dusty shafts, warming Sam's back as he sat at his writing desk. Smells of baking buttermilk biscuits and frying bacon drifted in from the kitchen, pleasantly teasing his empty stomach.

Sam heard footsteps. Before turning, he typed the date, June 17, 1927, on the cover letter for the article he had just finished.

Sam looked up. The doctor with his black bag soberly emerged from Mother's room and closed the door behind him. Dad and Don rose from the sofa, and Lucille came into the sitting room from the kitchen, drying her hands on a dish towel.

Sam knew in his heart that everything would be fine; Mom would be her old self again in a few days. Even though she was ill, she had seemed cheerful, happy, and serene. True, she had made a few attempts to speak to Sam about the possibility of her death, but Sam had immediately shushed these conversations with, "Oh, Mom, you'll be fine."

The doctor stepped up to Sam's father and stood regarding his old friend for a moment. "I'm sorry, Art. Kittie is dead."

Sam stood for a moment, unbelieving. Everything in his world disappeared; time stopped. He stood alone in a vast dark space, alone except for the beloved presence in the other room. He walked in a dream towards the bedroom door. Every step in the enormous darkness rang hideously in his ears, like a hammer on steel. He opened the door. The whining of the hinges as it swung open threatened to burst his eardrums. He looked down where his mother lay. Suddenly, he was alone, terribly alone, in the vast dark space, standing beside the bed. He did not know the person, or thing, on the bed. It was not Wegimind. Wegimind was gone, and with her, half of his soul.

He turned to flee the dark cavern with its horrible bed, but as he ran, the darkness stretched on and on.

Dad watched numbly as his younger son ran from the house. Even in his own shocked state, he felt himself worry about Sam. The young man had the capacity to hurt so deeply, and this was his first personal experience with death. How would he deal with the loss of his mother, whom he adored and idolized so much?

Sam ran until his breath was ragged and gasping. As he slowed to a walk, he began to recognize the streets and buildings around him. They looked different, somehow—as though he were seeing them through the eyes of a stranger. He was the stranger. Was he Sam Campbell? He felt different, the same but different, like an evil twin.

Evil, he thought. That's what causes death. I have seen evil face to face. His carefree and joyous spirit seemed to have been wiped away by the darkness, and his being filled with black bitterness and despair. Ugly emotions which had been mere abstractions for him until now suddenly appeared as intimate pieces of his soul. At his shocked recognition, they mocked him.

Some time later, Sam turned back toward the house. His heart was a cold weight in his chest. He knew what he must do. He had been deceived, Wegimind had been deceived. Life was not a happy, cheerful game. It was not the delicate scent of spring flowers, or the waters of a pristine lake sparkling in the summer sun. These were the pretty wrappings on the gift, but when the wrappings were happily torn away and the box opened, it was full of moldering decay and demonic laughter.

Sam knew he could not live in such a world. There was, after all his struggling to find his purpose in life, no purpose in life. He would refuse to live, to play this grotesque game, any longer.

Chapter Three

Bind Up the Broken-hearted

> *Oh, that I might spread this divine revelation over the grief-stricken hearts of the world!...The FATHER careth for us!*
>
> —*The Conquest of Grief*

Weak kneed, chests heaving with grief and despair, Sam and his father leaned against each other for support. The weeping cascades of a willow tree, quivering in the warm summer breeze, encircled the two men in an emerald canopy.

"I guess Wegimind would be pleased with this lot," Dad finally managed. His voice sounded old and hopeless. "Come on, Sam, let's buy this one and go home." He turned, suddenly a tired, bent old man, and began shuffling toward the car.

Home. The word stabbed Sam's chest like a dagger. There was no home; there would never again be a home, for Wegimind had died today. Waves of vertigo and nausea slammed against his body. He sank onto the thick green carpet of grass with a tortured gasp of fresh anguish. The azure sky, the golden sun warm on his face, the verdant green of growing things; all were horrible shades of gray to Sam, and the darkness pressed close about him as he lay on the ground in a fetal position, his arms convulsively encircling his knees.

Dad turned. The stark fear he suddenly felt for his son immediately cleared his own grief stricken, numbed brain. Although his own heart felt completely broken, his own eyes were full of bitter tears, and he only wished to live in order to care for his children, he recognized, in a sort of detached way, that his reactions were normal. Sam's pain, on the other hand, seemed impossibly horrible, as though all the griefs of the universe had been poured into his young soul. How could anyone, except characters in melodramatic paperback fiction, have the capacity to feel such anguish? He gently pulled his son to his feet and circled one of Sam's limp arms around his own neck, supporting the blindly staggering young man all the way back to their car.

Dad helped Sam into the passenger seat, then slid behind the wheel. As the car pulled out of the little country churchyard and began the drive back to the city, Sam's blinding, wrenching pain eased in a bittersweet haze of utter exhaustion. With a seeming clarity of thought, he recalled his resolution to end his own life. A sort of fateful sense of peace seemed to drug his senses as he stared out the window at the hypnotizing march of the roadside fences.

What! What could be happening? A sudden, glowing golden light appeared to radiate throughout the car! It penetrated Sam's darkened, numbed mind, and he snapped completely alert. His nightmarish state dissolved as Reality with its secure warmth seemed to flood his soul.

As Sam recorded in his diary:

We were silent, almost sullen, in our inward battle against grief and bitterness.

Suddenly the car in which we were driving, the road, and the countryside seemed to light with a most heavenly glow! It was as though the very weight of grief had cracked the confining walls of materiality, and a healing ray of Heaven burst through. I saw no vision, heard no voice, but felt myself inundated with a deluge of happiness, totally unlike that which comes from even the highest, worldly pleasures...

Oh, what words can I find that will tell the wild ecstasy of that precious moment? I think I did not breathe during the experience. I actually felt concern as to my sanity—then found immediate assurance that this, and this alone, was sane!

I looked about me. The world seemed to have stood still. The car lacked motion. The wayside trees possessed a new lustre which was apart from color. Marvelous beauty adorned the landscape, surpassing anything I have ever before seen. Particularly was I impressed with the beauty of one little bird which flew up from the road and lit on the fence. Though he was some distance off, and I had only a fleeting glimpse of him, it seemed as though he was right before my eyes, and stayed there indefinitely. I remember the brilliant marking of his plumage, which I might have called sombre under other circumstances. How conscious I felt of the omnipresence of LIFE! It was as though the WORD had been carved in my heart, so that I knew and saw nothing else. All this was outside of myself, and the experience seemed to hinge on my looking away and outward, for I had the sense that down somewhere within my own, erroneous thinking was all that which grieved me, and that it was my own creation!

How long this lasted I cannot say. All time seemed suspended and this vision of Reality bore no relationship to it. There was a sense of comfort in it which was supreme. Somehow it suggested a cool refreshing breeze on a torrid day, though the metaphor is woefully inadequate. It was then I saw that "death" is a deception, and grief was as impossible that moment with me as sin was with the MASTER!

I glanced at Father: then came the greatest joy! His face beamed with happiness! He, too, was living this sublime *experience! I shall never forget the heavenly expression of his countenance. I wondered if the happiness I felt was as apparent. We could not speak at the time, and later spoke only with difficulty, for human language offered no names for our experience. But we had the joy of corroboration, and by the slightest reference knew that our experiences had been the same. One outstanding fact was that in no way did this savor of the mysterious—it seemed divinely natural, as though this moment were predestined in creation.*

Dad and Sam soon reached the house, still elated by their marvelous experience. Relatives had already begun pouring in. One of Sam's first cousins who lived a day's drive from Chicago had just arrived. He had loved Wegimind dearly, but his face was strangely guarded. Sam wondered abstractly why his cousin's eyes did not betray the deep pain he must feel.

As Sam stepped forward to greet his cousin, he wondered with some trepidation if anyone noticed his own dry eyes and peaceful expression. He was half afraid the radiant joy in his heart would spill over onto his face and offend a mourner who did not understand. Sam hesitated as he came face to face with his cousin and recognized an unusual expression in his relatives's eyes.

The cousin must have seen something in Sam's face, too, because after a silent moment, he said, "Sam, come over here where we can talk. I have something I'd like to discuss. I have had an experience,—" He looked hesitantly at Sam, who was nodding knowingly, then went on to describe the very event which had happened to Sam and Dad! The cousin had had the same experience at the same time of day.

No sooner had his cousin gone on to talk with someone else than Sam's sister approached him with the same story! She had been doing housework at the time when the wonderful encounter occurred. Don also corroborated the experience.

The long day drew to a close. Sam sought out an empty room and sat down in an easy chair beside a window. He smiled as he heard laughter in the other room. Strange how the events of the day permitted laughter, and the lightheartedness of his own soul. The empty horror of the morning, his cold resolution to end his life, the glorious Presence he had felt in the car—all these scenes swirled through his mind as he tried to sort out the events of the day.

A strange shuffling, scratching noise intruded itself into Sam's thoughts. He looked down at the hardwood floor, and to his great astonishment saw the neighbor's dog, Count, crawling along the floor on his stomach toward the chair. The little mongrel had found an open door, and had come looking for his friend Sam. Count whined as he crawled right up to Sam's feet and began licking his shoes.

Sam lifted the flop-eared dog into his lap. Count pressed his hairy head with all his might against Sam's neck, and remained in that position for fully half an hour. Somehow the dog had empathically known his friend needed emotional support at this time.

Sam stroked the dog's wirey coat and stared out the window into the cold Chicago night. The stars were dimly visible. The wind whined mournfully through the window screen and rattled the glass. He turned from the dark scene and impulsively hugged the little brown dog.

"Count, with such love as this in the world, no sorrow can last long!"

Soon after Wegimind's death, Don, Dad, Lucille and Sam left for Three Lakes, Wisconsin. After camping on

Four Mile Lake for several summers, the Campbell family had eventually purchased a tidy cabin and some land along the west shore. Here the four now retreated to immerse themselves in creation, letting the summer sun bake, the wind scour, the rain rinse from their souls the tragedy of June.

The small cabin blending into the trees was full of happy memories. Sam could hear the laughter and singing, and could see his mother's smiling face at every turn. He half expected to feel a constant sorrow when faced with these phantoms from better days, but the roughly comfortable cabin, the woods and the lake, even the memories, comforted him.

Sam did feel the need to rest, but he mostly wished to isolate himself from the world for a time so he could think. He did not feel satisfied accepting the comfort of his spiritual encounter without vigorously pursuing a knowledge of the One he had encountered.

The Campbell family, though Christian, had not belonged to any particular denomination; they worshiped God under the deeply spiritual leadership of Wegimind, who was not comfortable with often divisive sectarianism. Although Sam had learned from his mother a deep awe of the majesty, beauty and goodness of God, he didn't have many theological roots.

Sam felt he must consolidate his spiritual experience with a coherent philosophy of life. He decided to withdraw from the working world for several months in order to spend many hours each day meditating, praying, and studying what the wise ones through the ages had written concerning the meaning of life. He would spend most of this time of solitude on the property up at Three Lakes. During these months, Sam read nearly all the great classics—the Bible, Emerson, Tolstoy, Whitman, Bergson, Tennyson, Dante, William

James—looking for descriptions of spiritual experiences such as his.

A strange transformation had come over Sam as he read about the love and manly gentleness of Jesus of Nazareth. He enjoyed the outdoors more than ever, but he began to see in nature certain revelations of God's character, and began to think of the wilderness as a house of worship. He not only lost his interest in hunting and trapping; he became repulsed by the thought of killing or injuring any living thing. Each life was a miracle to be marveled at and adored. He banned hunting and trapping on his land, and encouraged others to do the same.

Sam was sociable and extremely likable, but in some sense he had always been a bit of a loner, dreaming his own dreams and going his own ways. But now, even though he continued to cherish solitude and individuality, he began to see his fellow human beings in the same light he was seeing nature. Although he had always been a sensitive young man, he now felt new interest in the lives and cares of others.

As he learned more and more about God, he began to feel a mission to tell others, especially those in sorrow who had just lost a loved one, about the God of love and the healing He brings. The same spiritual leadership qualities so dominant in the character of Wegimind began to evidence themselves in Sam. He began to invite people over for hikes and campfire suppers. There was plenty of laughter and silliness at these gatherings, but Sam always endeavored to promote an overall atmosphere of spirituality and peace, and people always left his woodland home refreshed and blessed.

In honor of his mother, Sam decided to call the property on Four Mile Lake "The Sanctuary of Wegimind," for it had become a sanctuary for the worship of God, a sanctuary of protection for wildlife, and a sanctuary free from stress for the healing of tired and troubled human souls.

Sam soon began writing private and public letters of hope and encouragement which he sent to grieving people all over the world. His *Letters from the Sanctuary* became so well known and sought after that a friend offered to print them in book form for wider distribution. This was the first of Sam Campbell's books, *The Conquest of Grief*.

Also during this time, Sam wrote a series of philosophical nature essays known as the *Sanctuary Letters*. His friend printed these in individual booklets, each beautifully bound in richly-coloured velvet. *The Sanctuary of Wegimind*, *The Finding of Vanishing Lake*, *Ebony Mansions*, *Naturalness*, and *Frozen Memories* were full of rich descriptions of the north woods, and reflected Sam's growing philosophical convictions. These booklets were eventually included in Sam Campbell's book of essays, *Nature's Messages*.

Sam was still frustrated and confused about his career, or lack thereof, but he had at last found something he believed to be more fundamental than even a career; a philosophy of life, strong convictions, and a growing faith in God. And although wistful thoughts of his mother frequently brought tears to his eyes, no longer did death, destruction, and the power of evil bind his soaring soul.

Part Two

LIFE AT ITS BEST

1929–1962

SAM CAMPBELL Philosopher Of The Forest

Chapter Four

Scars of Our Folly

Everywhere we see the scars of our folly. Nor can we say that what our race did yesterday was foolish, but today we are wise. There seems to be only one wisdom and that is to interfere as little as possible with the natural order of things.
—*Nature's Messages*

It was late in the summer of 1929.

A lone birchbark canoe moved silently along the north shore of Four Mile Lake in the early morning light. A family of loons watched from the protective shadows of a small island a few hundred yards away. Occasionally one of the parent birds would lift its head and call out its haunting wail.

To the loons, the canoe appeared to be a log floating along the far bank, partially obscured by the mists rising from the warm water into the chilly morning air. The electric blue chamois shirt worn by the man who guided the craft seemed to the loons a piece of the sky come down to get a morning drink from the lake. They did not see the silent j-strokes, nor the little whirling vortices left behind by the broad blade of his paddle in the silky water.

The man's heavy khaki britches were tucked into high moccasin boots laced up to his knees. His prematurely graying, thinning brown hair ruffled in the slight breeze caused by the forward motion of the canoe. The movements of his powerful arms and broad chest were fluid and unhurried; he and his bark craft formed a perfectly natural part of the wild surroundings.

Sam felt the peace of the morning fill his soul. He nudged the bow of his canoe onto a short sandy beach, and lay back in the gently rocking craft, his face turned up towards the deepening blue of the morning sky. His eyes closed.

He could see himself standing there behind the lectern to one side of the wide, darkened stage. He could smell the varnish on the wooden flooring, the musty odor of the heavy velvet drapery cloaking the wings, the dust burning on the small light bulb which cast his typed narration notes in dim yellow light. He could see children in the front rows of the auditorium, their excited faces varying hues in the light reflected from the screen. Further back were dark outlines of more people, adults, unfamiliar presences filling the entire room. Over their heads hung a cone of light emanating from the projector far to the back of the auditorium. The beam was a collage of shifting colors filtering through lazily drifting motes of dust. He could hear the soothing hum of the projector, the clicking of the reels. He could hear his own voice, amplified by the narration microphone into strange resonances and cadences, filling every corner of the room.

A fat porcupine waddled onto the flickering screen. "Here's an old porcupine, his quills swaying back and forth like a load of hay as he walks. He has about 30,000 quills which he uses to protect himself. His tail can lash out with terrific speed, almost instantly embedding quills in an aggressor. Perhaps this gives rise to the false myth that porkies throw their quills.

"He's actually a fine, intelligent creature, but if one doesn't respect his unique prowess, he will prove the wisdom of that ancient adage: 'He who sitteth on a porcupine...'" Sam paused for effect, "shall rise again!" Loud laughter filled the hall. Sam could see the delighted faces of the children as they squealed out in raucous laughter. He could see careworn adult faces near the front splitting into happy grins. That simple little porcupine was for a few precious moments single handedly holding back the gloom of hard life in a big city.

"People haven't liked porkies very much because they are bark-eaters. They will sometimes live on a tree until they've girdled it completely—and then, of course, the tree dies. We must preserve porcupines, however, because they play their own unique and necessary role in nature. They actually thin out the forest so the remaining trees will be even stronger and healthier."

"We must preserve all these wild places and creatures which bring us so much pleasure. There must be places of great natural beauty where our young people can go to clear their heads of the world's meanness. We must protect wilderness, not only in order to preserve the physical conditions necessary for human life, but also in order to preserve the quiet sanctuaries necessary for the life of the human soul."

"It has been a great pleasure to be with you this evening. God bless you, and good night."

Applause rose in an almost deafening crescendo, but to Sam it seemed far away. His eyes were riveted on the children in the front rows, their eyes flashing with excitement as they jumped up and down, pointed at the now blank screen, and chattered to each other.

He stood there behind the lectern as the house lights came on and continued to watch the children as they rushed toward the stage, holding out their printed programs for autographs. *Here lies the future of the conservation movement, the future of the wilderness, the future of our world. If these little people are taught today how to love nature, what a difference it will make tomorrow!*

Sam sat up in the canoe, his blue eyes blinking in the bright morning light, but his mind was still far away in that darkened, dusty auditorium. He pushed away from the beach with his paddle, and began stroking along the shore once again.

Sam had spent the time since the death of his mother here at their cabin, reading, writing, studying nature, and learning how to operate the new moving picture equipment he had purchased. During this time, his developing philosophy of life had heavily influenced the way in which he saw the natural world. Nature had become a source of spiritual inspiration to him, and his new understanding of God's regard for every living thing had caused him to show new respect for the earth. He no longer hunted, littered, or thoughtlessly uprooted plants. As far as possible, he traveled through the wilderness without a trace, leaving everything in nature just as he had found it. He stepped around the tiny violets growing on the trail, and avoided trampling anthills. A half-joking rumor spread along the distant lakeshore cabins that Sam Campbell provided cotton for the mice in his house to use for nests! The neighbors would laugh fondly—they loved the humorous, kind man on Four Mile Lake—but they also shook their heads in wonder at his apparent eccentricity.

Sam had also joined the infant conservation movement, along with other far-sighted individuals who could see the terrible end result of human greed and exploitation of the planet. At that time in the "roaring twenties," conservation was hardly a popular notion; it would not become widely recognized until the ecology movement of the sixties, and even then would not become a vital concern of the general public until much later.

Concern for the future of his beloved wilderness and even the future of the planet encouraged Sam to produce a film of the flora and fauna of northern Wisconsin and a script to raise public awareness. He had shown his film in the Chicago area several times during the previous winter.

To Sam's surprise, these first nature lectures on the forests of northern Wisconsin had been a huge success. He had even attracted the attention of the Chicago and Northwestern Railway, who had contacted him about filming vacation advertisements for their northern rail destinations such as Eagle River and Three Lakes. Later, they hired him to lead tours through national parks.

Sam was beginning to realize that his writings would not, at least for some time, provide him with an adequate income. These lectures, on the other hand, could provide the bulk of an income... A plan was forming in Sam's mind; a vision of an exciting future of travel, wilderness exploration, nature study, writing, and lecturing. He would spend each summer in nature, filming his adventures and writing a story book about them, then he would travel about the country each winter showing his films, lecturing on nature and conservation, and selling his books.

The thought of such a life filled Sam's adventurous heart with joy! What a wonderful way to spend a happy life, and yet at the same time help protect the wilderness and be a service to others by providing them with wholesome entertainment and education.

Now that school had begun, the lecture season was fast approaching. Sam's summer days at the Sanctuary had come to a close. He recalled with a touch of apprehension that he was scheduled to give his first lecture of the season on the following Monday for a Chicago high school lyceum. He felt sure his new moving picture of wildlife antics was a good one, but the delicate balance of his finances and the lack of a steady income had given him a few sleepless nights lately, his excitement about his new career notwithstanding. Would he really be able to make ends meet?

Sam rounded a point of land, and headed for the homey brown and green cabin standing among the stately white pines along the shore. The morning mist was dissipating in the heat of the sun, now high over the eastern shoreline. The other-worldly mystery of the morning evaporated along with the fog as Sam's head filled with down-to-earth visions of a hearty breakfast of bacon and coffee. His dreams of the future, along with its nagging doubts and fears, vanished as he anticipated with pleasure the rugged work planned for the day.

Chapter Five

Think on These Things

> *For I am sure that beauty, power, balance, evenness are truly fundamental in nature. And I am equally sure that brotherly love, service, and Christian principles are basic with man. Human inventions inject all disturbances into both nature and man. "God hath made man upright; but they have sought out many inventions."*
>
> —*Nature's Messages*

Right after breakfast, Sam headed in to town to buy some groceries for the campfire supper he was planning with friends that evening.

By now the sun was high overhead and the sky had become a deep azure blue. A lazy breeze ruffled the surface of the lake as Sam rowed slowly toward the channel leading to Big Fork Lake. He had taken the comparatively sluggish rowboat instead of his sleek canoe because he knew he had to transport groceries back to the cabin.

He did not propel his craft with any great sense of purpose; in fact, a casual observer would not have guessed his ultimate destination to be the grocery store! He moved in a relaxed, unhurried way, as if he were determined to let the beauty of his surroundings soak into his very soul. His senses were alive with the movement and sound and color on every side.

His sharp eyes noticed the tall, narrow form of a great blue heron posing rigidly among the reeds along the western shoreline. He smiled delightedly at the mighty whoosh from the wings of a loon which flew close overhead on its way down the lake. He saw a large fish jump and watched the ring on the surface of the water expanding away toward shore.

In those days, no road led to the Campbell cabin. To reach town, Sam had to row down the length of Four Mile Lake, then turn southwest into the narrow channel which opened into neighboring Big Fork Lake. He kept his car parked at the public lake access on the eastern shore of Big Fork, right off Four Mile Creek Road.

The Thunder Lake Store on Highway 32 was about half way between Virgin and Whitefish Lakes, approximately four miles south of the landing where Sam kept his car. In the days when Sam and his family had first begun coming up from Chicago, the area was being heavily logged. This store belonged to Thunder Lake Lumber Company of Rhinelander, and was situated along a narrow gauge railroad which transported the felled timber. It was built as a depot to supply the logging camps to the north. As more people moved into the area, however, and as the logging of the region slowed, most of the store's business came from the local residents. The store was managed by a Three Lakes man named Cunningham. Sam knew who he was, of course, and had spoken to him many times when in his store for groceries.

Sam drove slowly along the winding, dusty track. He startled several deer, which darted across the road, white tails held high. A crow-sized pileated woodpecker flew its undulating path down the road in front of the car, looking for all the world like some prehistoric creature with its elevated red crest.

Sam turned left onto Highway 32 and drove past Virgin Lake. Soon the narrow road straightened, and a group of frame houses came into view. These were the homes built by the railroad for its employees. The midday sun shone down warmly as Sam parked the

Buick in the dusty lot by the lumber yard and boarding house, and walked across the road to the large two-story frame building beside the railroad tracks. The supply warehouses were in the back of this building, and the front was occupied by the grocery store.

He opened the front door of the store and stepped inside. The pleasantly cool interior seemed dim in contrast to the bright glare outside, and it smelled of spices and fresh vegetables.

Sam was greeted by a friendly man behind the counter. "Hello there! How are things over at Four Mile Lake?" the tall, trim man asked with a warm smile.

As Sam stood talking, three remarkably beautiful children trooped energetically through the door carrying school books and talking excitedly. The energy level of the room rose so dramatically, Sam wondered if he had suddenly been transported to the center of a hurricane or earthquake. The two little girls were of grade school age, slender, with lovely dark hair and eyes. The boy was a handsome, strong-looking lad in his early teens. "I'll bet there are Indians still living out there!" The older of the two girls looked very confident as she spoke.

"Oh, Jean, don't be silly! There are not." The boy rolled his eyes tolerantly at his sister's folly.

"Are there still Indians living out by Four Mile Lake, Daddy?" the younger girl called out. "One of our friends at school said so." Three pairs of expectant eyes turned to the man.

"This gentleman lives on Four Mile. Why don't you ask him?" The grocer turned mischievous eyes on his smiling customer.

Sam squatted down to the younger childrens' level, and smiled broadly. The children felt drawn to this stranger's open, kind face and friendly manner. Their expectant eyes fixed on his.

To give himself time to think, Sam said "Well, I'm sure you know of the Potawatomi Indian John Shabodock who lives near here. He's a real chief. Sometimes he comes into town." The children nodded, but were still waiting for the answer to their question.

"But are there Indians still living out at Four Mile Lake?" Sam paused, noting the bated breath and hopeful expressions. Even the boy looked hopeful! "You know, I feel very sad when I think about how we white people took away all their land and cut down their ancient trees." Sam's face had become solemn. He felt he should take the opportunity to inject a note of reality. The children looked distressed. Sam continued more cheerfully:

"Well, I do know that not so long ago a real Indian named Ben lived in a small shack in that little clearing on the north shore. In fact, I've spoken to Ben. He told me stories about a wolverine that used to visit his cabin. So, I guess if an Indian lived there just a few years ago, it is possible that there may be another Indian still living in the area."

It was the right thing to say! The children were looking at Sam as if he were the Indian from Four Mile Lake! Sam recognized in the childrens' rapt expressions the awe and longing for adventure and wilderness which he had felt at their age, and which he admittedly still felt. Sometimes as a boy he had wished so much for wilderness that he had literally become sick.

"I'm Sam. What are your names?"

The older girl smiled with importance. "I'm Jean Cunningham, this is my little sister Beth, and this is my brother Howard. My Dad runs this place."

The father proffered his hand to Sam. "You know, we've known of each other for several years, but we never have really introduced ourselves. I'm Roy, and you've just met the children."

"I'm Sam Campbell. Our family has come up here pretty much every summer to vacation for the last 17 years. But I'm going to be living here from now on except for a few of the winter months."

They stood there talking easily for a long time. LeRoy Cunningham knew a lot about the history of the area. He had been a railroad dispatcher in Wausau and Antigo before moving with his family to Three Lakes in 1920 to manage the supply depot.

When there was a natural lull in the conversation, Roy Cunningham said, "Say, Sam, why don't you come over to the house and meet my wife Ida? It's just down the road from here. Howard, would you watch the store for a few minutes? I'll be right back."

Sam quickly collected his groceries, and went with Roy and the two girls to the Cunningham home. Ida Cunningham was gracious and kind, and Sam had an overwhelming sense that he already knew these sweet people as close friends. He was surprised at how comfortable and at ease he felt in their presence.

"We hear you've banned hunting and trapping on your land." Ida spoke up.

Sam nodded. "Yes, I've come to the place where I don't get any joy out of hunting or trapping anymore. In fact, it's becoming difficult for me to understand how I ever considered it 'sport' to kill defenseless animals." Sam spoke frankly, without any tone of condemnation. "Besides, I'm a wildlife photographer, and I want word to get around in animal society that my land is a safe place." For a moment Sam wondered if these people might find his aversion to hunting offensive, as did many of the locals. But he thought he read approval in their eyes.

As Sam was getting ready to leave, it felt completely natural to invite these new friends over to the Sanctuary that evening for the campfire supper. The Cunninghams seemed delighted by the invitation, and when all the necessary arrangements had been made, Sam returned with his groceries to Four Mile Lake to finish the day's work and prepare for his guests.

The sun went down that evening in a brilliant array of colors. The glassy surface of Four Mile Lake was stained with shifting shades of gold, baby blue, pink, purple, and forest green. A thin, vertical column of smoke rose like a flag, welcoming the four canoes entering the far end of the lake. As they approached, they could make out the leaping orange flames of the campfire along the shore, and the form of Sam Campbell as he stacked a load of wood near the fire pit.

As soon as Sam noticed the canoes floating on the colored tapestry of the lake, he waved happily and called out to them. Sam Campbell's guests always felt welcomed. The way he focused all his attention on the one he was greeting made that person feel like the most important person in the world.

The campfire supper was a huge success, and everyone seemed to have a genuinely good time. There was lots of good food and easy conversation, and certainly no lack of entertainment. The three Campbell men made sure of that! The Cunninghams could see how Dad, Don and Sam Campbell had gotten their reputation for crazy jokes, teasing, and hilarious conversation.

The giggling of the Cunningham children repeatedly punctuated the happy babble as Sam took every opportunity to tease them. Most adults have a way of ignoring children when they are with other adult friends, but Sam Campbell made the children feel like members of the circle as he listened to their comments and frequently addressed remarks to them.

When the baked beans, hotdogs, popcorn, and cake had all disappeared and everyone was lounging comfortably in the warm circle of firelight, Sam produced his guitar.

"This guitar has been around Hunter Island, you know," Sam said as he fondly patted the slightly battered instrument.

At this announcement, several of the guests looked up with interest. The Cunningham children looked especially curious. They were clearly waiting to hear more.

"Way up in Minnesota," Sam began, his eyes sparkling with excitement, "on the very border of the United States and Canada, lies a vast roadless wilderness called the Quetico-Superior 'canoe country.' There is nearly more water there than land, and the only efficient way to travel in the summer is by canoe. Canoe country is the land made famous by the travels of the French-Canadian Voyageur fur traders, who paddled with their merchandise along those lake and river 'highways.'"

"In those days, one of the main routes lay along what is today the international boundary. Another main route was farther north, going from Saganaga, through Kawnipiminicock and Sturgeon Lakes, and into Lac La Croix. The area in between these two major waterways is called 'Hunter Island.' I'll be going there again, soon, I hope. You can really find solitude up there!"

"Let me teach you a Voyageur chanson," Sam continued. "The voyageurs sang as they paddled, and they sang around their campfires at night. They were rugged, carefree, and loved to sing."

Sam strummed a few introductory chords on his guitar, then he, Dad and Don began singing vigorously in French,

En roulant ma boule roulant,
En roulant ma boule.
Derrier' chez nous, yatun etang,
En roulant ma boule.
Trois beaux canards s'en vont baignant,
Rouli, roulant, ma boule roulant.
En roulant ma boule roulant,
En roulant ma boule.

The rollicking melody of "A-rolling My Ball" was easy to learn and fun to sing, and soon the group was confidently learning another verse.

They sang other songs, too. "There Is a Long, Long Trail Awinding," "O Danny Boy," "Tenting Tonight," and "Open Mine Eyes" floated over the water. For over an hour, their songs echoed across the black lake, mingling with the sounds of the night. Finally, they sang,

When you come to the end of a perfect day,
And you sit all alone with your thought,
While the chimes ring out with a carol gay,
For the joy that the day has brought.

Do you think what the end of a perfect day,
Can mean to a tired heart,
When the sun goes down with a flaming ray,
And dear friends have to part?

Well, this is the end of a perfect day,
Near the end of a journey, too,
And it holds a thought that is big and strong,
With a wish that is kind and true.

*For memory has painted this perfect day,
In colors that never fade,
And we find at the end of a perfect day,
The soul of a friend we've made!*

When the last chords had faded away, the small group sat in comfortable silence for several long minutes, staring into the orange flames.

A young man finally broke the reverie in low tones. "Sam, how can we explain all the pain and suffering in the world? What about hatred and meanness and war? How can a loving God permit these things?"

Sam reflected quietly for a moment before he spoke. This perceptive young friend had just verbalized the question which had sent Sam to the depths of despair, and then on a redemptive spiritual journey, scarcely two years before.

"Well," Sam began slowly, choosing his words carefully. "I cannot explain why living creatures feel pain. Nor can I explain why the plants and even the inanimate natural beauties of this earth suffer destruction and ruin, often from the hand of man. I do, however, believe that destruction, pain, meanness and hatred are not the truly natural order of things. In the truly natural universe, the truly real universe, order, harmony, peace, and happiness are the rule, because these are the traits of the Creator."

Sam paused. A barred owl called its distinctive eight hoots from somewhere in the region of Four Mile Creek.

"This appears to leave something of a contradiction, I know," he continued slowly. "I can only conclude that the world as we perceive it is unnatural and, in some sense, unreal. We are not seeing the entire picture."

The young questioner looked up at Sam for a moment before turning his gaze back to the fire. His brow furrowed in thought as he stared into the depths of the dancing flames. "So how can we cope with this day-to-day, unnatural world?"

Sam nodded to show he understood the question. "My sweet mother died two years ago last June. I thought I would die from the grief." He paused, remembering. "Then I was blessed to be given a very real encounter with the presence of the Divine. In His presence, the darkness fled from my soul. I still didn't understand the pain, but God's presence was enough. It was the true Reality."

"In the biblical story of Job, Job's wife and friends all discussed the subject of suffering and gave the popular answers of the day. They said that since Job was suffering so terribly, he must have done something wrong, and God was punishing him."

"But at the end of the story, God Himself showed up and rebuked the friends for their false portrayal of His character. He reminded Job that human vision of life is very limited and distorted, and reminded him of the power and enormity of God. In the end, Job found the true reality of life to be in God's presence."

"So when we have the divine Presence with us, we learn to live by the truly natural rules of the universe. Scripture counsels us to dwell on things that are true, honest, just, pure, lovely, and of good report. 'If there be any virtue, and if there be any praise, think on these things.'"

Sam spoke earnestly, without any hint of embarrassment. "I believe that faith means a conviction, a trust deep down in the heart, that God is completely good and loving, and that His universe runs on the law of kindness. When we allow love to rule in our hearts as Jesus Christ did, we begin to enter into Reality as citizens of the heavenly kingdom."

Think on These Things

The group sat for some time in reflective silence. The diamond stars shining through black arms of fir and spruce, the gentle lapping of wavelets onto the beach, and the distant wail of a loon added spiritual power to Sam's words.

Although it was time to leave, no one wished to interrupt the powerful mood of the night. One by one, the guests said soft goodbyes and slipped quietly away into the darkness. The Cunninghams lingered for a while around the fire after the others had gone.

"Sam," Roy Cunningham said earnestly, "the things you said tonight were insightful. Do you belong to a particular church?"

Sam shook his head. "Not yet, but I've looked into several, and have found one which seems to most closely match my own convictions." He named a small but vigorous denomination. "I've been going to the local church near my home in Chicago. Do you happen to know if there's one in this area?"

Roy and Ida looked surprised, then glanced at each other and smiled. Ida said warmly, "Why, yes, we do; there's one in Eagle River. That happens to be our home church! Would you like to go with us this Sunday?"

Sam Campbell didn't fully realize it that evening around the campfire, but he had entered a new era of fulfillment in his life. He would find a fellowship of Christians, a church home, in the little white frame building on the corner of 3rd and Pine in the nearby town of Eagle River. And in the Cunninghams, he would find another home; true, lifelong friends who became as beloved as family.

Chapter Six

Land of the Voyaguers!

> *The larger lesson of a world depression is that we should make a distinction between financial values and real values...Spiritual values are the real ones, and life conducted on any other basis is as a "house built upon the sands." The presence of fabulous wealth has never given happiness where it has been gained at the sacrifice of character. Ultimately, investment will be judged from only one standpoint: its contribution to mental progress and peace of mind.*
>
> —*Nature's Messages*

"Sam!" Bobby grabbed his friend's shoulders and shook them with enthusiastic abandon. "Hello in there! Let's get the stuff in the car! Let's GO!"

Sam smiled warmly at his young companion, then closed his eyes and briefly shook his head. "Well, Bobby old pal, I guess you could say I'm getting cold feet." He surveyed the mound of gear still piled in the rowboat. "Do you realize I've spent my last cent on this trip? We barely have enough money to buy gas for the car on the way up and back. By the time we get back, if we get back," he cast Bobby an amused glance, "I won't have a penny to my name."

It was summertime, early 1930's. The "Roaring Twenties" had collapsed on Black Thursday, October 24, 1929, into the Great Depression. Times were hard, and fear of the future lined every face. Chicago was gloomy and full of pessimism. Even the town of Three Lakes, deep in the magical wooded northlands, felt economic hardship. "Moonshining" was rampant and tolerated, and there were fights in the streets.

Land of the Voyaguers!

But here in the forest Sanctuary where Sam lived and worked, life went on much as usual. The uncounted lakes and streams, the trees swaying in the wind, the fishing raccoons and diving loons, the snorting deer and lumbering bear—all these were oblivious to the financial disaster. As was a certain excitable young man.

"Come on, Sam, you're a worry wart. You're smart enough to figure the money out later." He pretended to look at Sam critically. "Well, maybe you're not that smart...but at least you know enough about edible wild plants to live off the land. Sam, if we don't leave soon, we won't reach Ely before the boarding house closes for the night!"

"OK, let's go, Bobby." Sam shrugged, and rolled his eyes in mock resignation at Dad and Don, who stood nearby on the dock. As he finished lashing the canoe to the roof of the car, and loaded the gear from the rowboat into the trunk and backseat, he muttered, "Go ahead and send me to the poor house. You can come visit me there sometimes..."

"Huh?" Bobby poked his head out of the back seat where he was arranging the packs. "What did you say, Sam?"

"I said it's about time we got on the road! Why don't you hurry up? You're making us late!" Sam grabbed the steering wheel and swung into the driver's seat. Bobby jumped into the passenger seat and slammed the door with unnecessary vigor, his face glowing with excitement.

"'Bye Dad, 'bye Don! We'll see you in about a month!" Sam and Bobby waved their arms through the open windows of the Buick as Sam smoothly let in the clutch and headed the car down Four Mile Lake Road towards the town of Three Lakes.

Bobby Kostka was a young man in his late teens, tall and thin, with wavy light brown hair and laughing blue eyes. He was a member of the Octagon Club, the study group for teenagers at Sam's church. Sam was one of sponsors of this group, and Bobby was one of several young people in the Club who became involved in helping with Sam's nature work.

Early on, Sam recognized this bright, enthusiastic young man as a potentially talented naturalist. Bobby became Sam's assistant, helping with photography, working with the animals, and accompanying Sam on some of his lecture tours. When Sam decided to go back to the Quetico to gather material for a new lecture film, he invited this young man along on whose help he had come to rely.

Sam and Bobby drove north from Three Lakes on U.S. Highway 45 for about forty miles to Watersmeet in the Upper Peninsula of Michigan. From here, U.S. Highway 2 winds west just south of Lake Superior for about 180 miles to Duluth, Minnesota.

It was early afternoon by the time Sam and Bobby reached Duluth. They drove up the steep coastal incline and stopped the car for a moment to look down on the cities of Duluth and Superior where they perched along the side of the blue freshwater sea stretching away into the horizon.

"How much further to Ely?" Bobby leaned back against the car in the warm sunshine and stretched contentedly.

"Oh, about 125 more miles, I'd say. About three hours away. They're expecting us at the boardinghouse for supper."

"By the way, exactly what is this boardinghouse? Who lives there, just tourists to the area?"

Land of the Voyaguers!

Sam's cheerful face took on a faraway look. "No, actually it's a boardinghouse for the lumberjacks who are logging that country."

"Logging the canoe country? You mean the trees will all be cut down where we're going?" Sam felt a secret satisfaction at the alarmed look on his young friend's face. No, he had not misjudged Bobby as an outdoor companion. Not only was the lad a good woodsman; he was also truly in love with nature.

As Sam was beginning to realize, the blessing one receives from an outdoor journey depends a great deal on one's companions. People who complain about rain, mud, hunger, plain food, mosquitoes, biting flies, and all the other discomforts of wilderness travel have a way of spoiling nature's compensations of rainbows, hearty appetites, and quiet evenings around the campfire. On the other hand, cheerful companions who enjoy the challenge of hardship without complaint, who always point out the interesting and the beautiful, who love all of nature's moods, make an outing a glorious adventure.

It's easiest to travel through such country with an even number of people, so that each canoe has someone at bow and stern. Sam knew it would be safer to go in a party of at least four so the group would have two canoes, but he was longing for a deeper solitude. He had decided that he and Bobby would go alone on this trip. Besides, the two of them would have to spend a lot of their time on photography.

"Sam!" Sam jerked out of his revelry to find Bobby's face glaring at him, inches from his own. "You better fork up some grub if you don't wanna get rubbed out." The imitation of a Chicago mafia boss was laughable coming from the thin faced, blue-eyed young man with the perpetual smile.

Sam's face lit with amusement as though he had just thought of something funny. "Well, there's a hotdog stand over there, my friend, but I advise temperance."

"What do you mean? Aren't they safe to eat?" Bobby looked suddenly alarmed at the prospect of going hungry.

"Oh, yes, I'm quite sure they're fine hotdogs, maybe the best of their breed. But as your friend, I must warn you not to..."

But Bobby had already walked over to the stand, and was handing money over in exchange for a huge bag of fat, beefy hotdogs, each smothered in ketchup, mustard, and onions, and encased in a large whole wheat bun.

"Here, Sam. You can have one if you promise to speed up and get us there in time for supper."

"No, thanks. I'll just wait 'til we get to Ely. And I really doubt you will want me to speed up any." Sam was starting the engine, and Bobby flopped into the passenger seat with his precious bag of hotdogs, eying Sam suspiciously. Why was he being so mysterious, and what had happened to that legendary Campbell appetite?

They left Duluth driving northeast on U.S. Highway 61, which follows the rugged, hilly northern coast of Lake Superior. They continued on Highway 61 until just past the town of Silver Bay, where they took State Highway 1 northwest toward the tiny logging settlement of Ely, Minnesota. Sam wrote, "Through hours we wrestled with its twists and turns, its hills and valleys, as though it were a great serpent which we must bring into subjection."

Bobby had wolfed down all the sandwiches before they even left Duluth's city limits, despite Sam's continued mysterious warnings. Whenever Bobby would demand to know the reason why he should go hungry, he would only get a solemn shake of the head, and the admonition, "Just trust me, my friend."

"Well, Bobby, old buddy." Sam yawned and stretched behind the wheel. "I guess we're finally on the 'long, winding road to Ely.' By the way, how's your stomach?"

Bobby's face was pale, and there was a sheen of moisture on his forehead. "My stomach's OK. Why, what do you mean?" Bobby gave Sam a weak smile. "You didn't think I'd get car sick, did you?"

"Hmmm. I guess you wanted me to hurry, didn't you, so we would get to supper on time." Sam bore down harder on the gas pedal, and the Buick sped around the tight curves with unnecessary speed.

"Sam!" Bobby's voice was desperate. "Stop! I need to stop!"

Anyone who has ever felt the griping nausea of car sickness will understand how Bobby felt, and will know just exactly what he did when Sam stopped the car.

Sam stood by with concern; he hadn't really expected his friend to get so sick.

"I'll get you back for this one, friend Sam." Bobby clearly felt much better after having gotten rid of the offending hotdogs, and was goodnaturedly taking advantage of Sam's obvious repentance. "When I'm the cook in camp, I won't bother to call you when the chow's ready. I'll make you forage for mushrooms and berries."

"Are you feeling well enough to ride again?" Sam inquired worriedly.

"No, I think I'll just walk for a while, thank you."

During the remainder of the drive, Bobby often had to get out and walk, much to his chagrin. He really did wish he hadn't eaten those hotdogs, and by the time they reached the boardinghouse at Ely late in the afternoon, he had no interest at all in eating the hearty supper which the landlady spread out for them.

Early the next morning before sunrise, Sam awakened Bobby, and they drove a little further north to the tiny town of Winton. Winton was a settlement of a few hundred Finnish lumberjacks, perched precariously on the border of civilization and wilderness. It was as far north as one could drive an automobile in this part of the country.

The morning's destination was the four-year-old Border Lakes Outfitting Company on Fall Lake, partly owned by Sigurd F. Olson of Ely. Sam had met the Olson family when he first came to canoe country several years before. Sig Olson was well-known nationally as a writer, teacher, geologist and eloquent conservationist, besides being a famous guide of the Quetico. He and Sam had struck up an immediate friendship, and had taken some memorable trips together through the vast wilderness to the north.

Before long, Sam and Bobby pulled up in front of the large, roughly hewn frame warehouse. Sam felt a deep excitement stir within himself as he got out of the car and surveyed the view. Fall Lake, sparkling in the first rays of the rising sun, filled the background of the scene with a bold wash of blue. They pushed open the door of the warehouse and stepped inside.

The large room was cool and dim on the inside, and smelled of canvas and varnish. Scores of canoes rested on racks hung from the rafters. Packsacks, paddles, and lifejackets hung on the wall. Cooksets, fire grates, canteens; everything a canoe camper needed were stacked neatly on shelves. Sam watched Bobby's face light up with excitement. This was the kind of place which always made Sam's heart beat fast.

Land of the Voyaguers!

"Sam Campbell!", yelled two teenage boys in unison from across the warehouse. "Dad, Sam Campbell is here!" Sigurd, Jr, and Robert Olson, Sig's sons, were sandy haired, rugged youths. Sam knew these boys were already excellent outdoorsmen in the tradition of their father. They had taken a great liking to Sam on his previous visits, and the affection was mutual.

"Hello, Sig! Hello Bob! My goodness, you two have really grown up!" Sam wrapped the boys in a quick bear hug. "I want you to meet my friend Bobby Kostka. Well, if it isn't the bourgeois himself!"

A tall man had appeared from behind a rack of canoes. He was a Scandinavian, lean and darkly tanned. His face was alight with a big smile of welcome. "Welcome, Sam! How are you?" He gripped Sam's hand firmly.

Sig Olson was known in these parts as the bourgeois. The designation was high praise indeed, for it was the name the Voyageurs gave their leaders.

"We have everything you requested all ready to go, Sam," Sig Olson said. "A Duluth pack and raingear for Bobby, a fire grate, and this waterproof packsack for your camera equipment. You remember John Sanstead, one of our guides? He's going to tow you up Fall Lake and Basswood Lake to the Canadian ranger station, where you'll have to stop to go through customs. Then he'll take you on up to Bayley Bay and drop you off. OK? Let's look over your route before you go."

Sam and Sig spread a large map out on Sig's desk, and began discussing the various pros and cons of the route Sam had tentatively planned. Sig's intimate knowledge of the region was invaluable: this lake had better fishing, that lake was more likely to have moose, such and such portage was completely overgrown, on a certain cliff were prehistoric Indian pictographs, this river was now blocked by beaver dams.

While the two men pored over the map, Bobby and the Olson boys packed Bobby's gear into the Duluth pack, and carefully packed the camera equipment. Then they carried all the gear and Sam's canoe out to the dock where the tow launch bobbed up and down on incoming wavelets.

Sam and the guide soon came out of the warehouse and down to the dock. Sam mentally checked off the list of things they needed. Sam's pack, Bobby's pack, camera pack, food and cookware (distributed in Sam and Bobby's packs), tent (strapped to the top of Sam's pack), fire grate, sleeping bags, fishing gear, maps, tarpaulin (strapped to the top of Bobby's pack), Sam's guitar—everything was in order.

"Taking your guitar again, I see," commented the guide as he began tying the canoe to the launch.

"Sure, I never leave home without it." Sam smiled somewhat guardedly. He was used to being ridiculed for this flagrant departure from the tradition of traveling light.

"Well, I used to would have said it was crazy, you taking that bulky guitar, especially when you are having to take all that heavy camera stuff. But I remember how nice it was to have along." John Sanstead looked at Bobby Kostka and the Olson boys.

"I guided Sam a few years ago on that trip he took up to Kahnipiminanikok. We had to portage around a whole string of falls on the way up, and I remember just dreading having to carry that guitar around each one. But I was won over pretty quickly; singing around the campfire every night was a real treat. I'll never forget that trip. It was one of the best I've ever guided."

When the mound of luggage was secured on the launch, the guide coaxed the sputtering engine to life and loosed the moorings. They were off! The guide took them up the length of Fall Lake, over Long Portage, the four mile truck portage, and into Hoist Bay.

Hoist Bay is the southern most reach of huge Basswood Lake. The Voyageurs called this lake Lac du Bois Blanc, or "Whitewood Lake," using the French word for the basswood tree.

Large rollers, driven by a stiff breeze, marched down the east arm of Basswood as the trio headed up the lake toward the Canadian Ranger Cabin. The air was filled with flying foam and spray as the launch cut through the oncoming waves.

"I sure am glad you're towing us up Basswood today," Sam shouted over the gale. "We might have been windbound in Hoist Bay, otherwise. In fact, I haven't seen any canoes out on Basswood so far today."

John Santead nodded. "You certainly wouldn't want to paddle upwind on Basswood today. The waves can get pretty big out here. You know, I got caught out here one day when a bigger wind than this came up. I was guiding a party of two canoes up to some of the best fishing spots in Hunter Island. A man and his wife, both college professors, were in one canoe, and the other man, a carpenter as I remember, was in the bow of my canoe. Fortunately, all three of them were experienced canoeists."

"Anyway, we were quartering the waves as best we could, and our canoes were separated by maybe a hundred feet. People don't believe me when I tell them this next part, but it's true. I'll never forget looking over where the other canoe was supposed to be, and not seeing it! I was afraid they had capsized, but in a moment I saw their canoe climb up on the next wave, then we went down in a trough, and I lost sight of them again! When the waves are so high you lose sight of a canoe right next to you, you shouldn't be out there!" The guide shook his head in wonder at the experience.

About half way up the lake, they stopped at a small island on the Canadian border and checked through customs at the ranger station. By the time the launch reached Bayley Bay at the northern end of this arm of Basswood, the sun had long since passed its zenith. Sam decided they should go ahead and make camp on Basswood Lake that night, then portage out first thing in the morning.

The guide dropped Sam and Bobby off with their gear at a nice campsite in the bay, and headed back at high speed in order to reach Border Lakes Outfitting Company by dark.

Sam and Bobby filmed the departing launch, then set about making their first camp. The last party had thoughtfully left their tentpoles leaning against a tree, and had covered a stack of firewood with birchbark to keep it dry. Bobby filmed Sam pitching the canvas tent and doing other camp chores.

Before they had left Winton, Sam had gone down to the lakeshore and rigged up a scene for a special film segment. He tied several lengths of clear line to the bow, stern, and gunwales of the canoe, then ran the line through carefully placed pulleys in the trees overhead. While the Olson boys pulled on the lines, Bobby filmed a hilarious segment of Sam and his canoe dancing with joy in the shallow water! This film would later be spliced in between scenes of the departing launch and the sequence of setting up camp.

Even though the rigged celebratory dance had already taken place, Sam couldn't help whirling around the stone fireplace a few times with unrestrained joy.

Land of the Voyaguers!

"We're here, Bobby! We're really here!" panted Sam as he dropped to the ground beside the blaze and began setting out supper. He grinned widely at Bobby, who grinned right back with equal enthusiasm. In fact, Bobby hadn't stopped grinning since he had awakened that morning. "And tomorrow we will portage into the Quetico. No more motors, very few people, just wilderness!"

Early the next morning, they portaged into Burke Lake, then around the falls at the northern end of Burke into the North Bay of Basswood Lake, where they stopped for lunch.

By early afternoon, they had reached long, narrow Isabella Lake, where they were to make camp.

That night when they had crawled into their sleeping bags in the tent, Sam was wakeful. He lay there staring at the canvas ceiling, listening to the night sounds and wondering what strange events might be transpiring in the forest. Bobby fell asleep quickly, and his loud snoring soon filled the air, drowning out most of the forest symphony.

Unable to fall asleep, Sam finally got dressed and quietly slipped out of the tent. He followed a path through the moonlit forest, stopping every so often to listen to the night. The path stopped at the margin of a beaver pond. Sam sat down on a log to watch.

The beavers, ignoring the extra shadow which had appeared on shore, industriously swam back and forth in the moonlight carrying their loads of sticks.

Sam watched this wilderness performance in awe for some time. Suddenly, he heard a movement in the brush nearby. He turned. To his astonishment, a large beaver was walking purposefully toward him!

Sam froze. He expected that at any moment the beaver would see him and run away, but the beaver kept coming. It was soon apparent to Sam that not only did the beaver see him, it was intent on walking right up to him!

Sam felt as if he were in another world as that citizen of the wilderness stopped right at his feet and looked up calmly into his face. Sam was sure the experience could not possibly become more intense, when suddenly the beaver raised up and rested his front feet on Sam's knee! In this position he stood for several minutes, looking intently into Sam's face as though he were trying to communicate.

Finally, the beaver lowered himself to the ground, and unhurriedly walked to the pond, where he slipped quietly into the black water and swam away.

Sam had never been so excited! He knew he wouldn't be sleeping at all that night. After returning to camp, he built a small fire in the rock fireplace, and sat looking out over Isabella Lake. Why had nature decided to initiate him into her secret society? He felt the beaver experience had some deep significance for his life, if only he could pinpoint it.

Although by far his most remarkable experience, this was not the first time he had been the recipient of friendly gestures from wild creatures of late. In the last few years, he had felt a dramatic change in his relationship with the wilderness. As he sat there on the banks of Isabella, he struggled to understand.

Attitude, he finally realized as the first rose of dawn streaked the sky. My attitude has changed. When I hunted and destroyed animals, they did not trust me. I did not have experiences like this. Now that my attitude is no longer threatening, I am gaining the confidence of wild creatures.

Land of the Voyaguers!

The days passed in happy succession, each with its own extraordinary joys. They spent several days in beautiful Sarah Lake, one of Sam's favorites, explored the shores of McIntyre Lake, passed through Brent and Conmee Lakes, and slogged across the long portages into large Pooh Bay Lake during a downpour. Two more portages brought them to the Malign River, on the northern perimeter of Hunter Island.

They filmed bear on Sturgeon Lake, and moose on the Malign river. They fished the waters of Lac La Croix while windbound there for several days, and filmed the roaring cataract of Curtain Falls. They examined the ancient Indian pictographs on Picture Rock of Crooked Lake, and portaged around the treacherous falls of the Basswood River, where so many of the Vogageurs' canoes were lost.

On their last night in the Quetico, Bobby and Sam sat in front of a friendly, crackling campfire on the west arm of Basswood Lake. Their conversation turned to the mystery of the beaver experience, and to all the other magical moments of the journey.

"These are the real values, Bobby," said Sam with conviction. "Peace, progress in understanding spiritual truths, recognition and love of beauty, a natural lifestyle, honest friendship, an apprehension of God's presence. During these last few weeks, we have been in touch with what is real. All the woes of the stock market, all the disasters of the financial world, cannot take these things from us. We spent nearly our last penny to make this trip, but it will be one of the best and most productive investments ever made."

Chapter Seven

Spirit of the Wilderness

> *(After my first visit to this area as a boy), never could I forget the effect that vast forest had on my thought...The forest exceeded anything I had pictured in my dreams. It was ancient, immense, mysterious, captivating. I felt as if there were some all-pervading force encompassing it. This I named the Spirit of the Wilderness, referring to the unbroken, primitive atmosphere.*
>
> —*Moose Country*

Long before white people arrived to carve their scars into the wilderness of upper Wisconsin, Ojibway, Chippewa, and Potawatomi Indians lived and hunted inconspicuously in the primeval forests. Like the people of all human civilizations, their lives were shaped by births, deaths, love, family, and friendships, by industry and survival, and by religion, patriotism, war, diplomacy, and community. They did differ, however, in a few important ways from the white newcomers which would eventually drive them from the land of their ancestors.

In general, possessions, wealth, and greed did not motivate these people. They appreciated the things the earth gave them, and took only what they needed from the land. Although they built villages and in general lived comfortably, they did not feel the white people's fear of wilderness, and felt no need to conquer, subdue, and banish it from their daily lives. The Indians did not insulate themselves from the outdoors; they became intimate with it. They lived in harmony with wilderness, knew its every mood, understood its secrets, traveled its vast, trackless halls.

Long ago, some of these native peoples settled in a particularly rich hunting and fishing ground along the shores of a certain chain of crystal lakes, near what is today Nicolet National Forest. Their villages and camps along the shores of these waters were filled daily with laughing children and industrious activity. Could the Indians have observed their homes from the air, they would have seen a sprawling necklace of sparkling jewels nestled in a dark velvet expanse of vast, dense forests.

This ancient waterway consisted of twenty-eight medium sized lakes, all connected by navigable channels, with myriad peripheral lakes and flowages. Immense conifer forests of huge trees covered the surrounding low, gently rolling hills. Dank muskegs shivered in the valley floors, vanishing remnants of ancient lakes left behind by the retreating glaciers. In some valleys, diminutive patches of open water ringed by encroaching sphagnum still looked up from the centers of soggy tarns as if to gaze one last time upon the sky above before disappearing forever.

Roving packs of wolves watched shyly from the brush as the graceful birchbark canoes of the Indians moved silently along these shores in the morning mists. Huge bull moose with their great racks of horns, and cows with gangly calves grazed the marshy shallows. At dusk, shrieks of mountain lions echoed through the deep woods, paralyzing the denizens of those dark shades.

By the 1860's, white settlers had established trading posts in the Eagle River and Three Lakes areas. Daniel Gagen and Hiram "Hi" Polar were well known white traders who bartered with the local Indians in those days. A village of several hundred Chippewa Indians and a handful of white families quickly grew up around the flourishing trading center which would eventually become the town of Three Lakes. The government of the

United States began granting land in the area to homesteaders during the mid 1880's.

In 1881, the Milwaukee, Lakeshore and Western Railway (later the Chicago and Northwestern Railway) tried to run a line north through the area, but the surveyor found a lake in the way on each of his three attempts. Most of the area was still a dense wilderness, and the surveyor did not know of the scores of other lakes dotting the landscape. Because of these three lakes (Maple, Townline, and Rangeline Lakes) encountered by the surveyor, the town was named Three Lakes.

One of the more isolated lakes of the chain was known as Four Mile Lake. This lake lay to the east of the main waterway. Its only connection to the chain was a navigable channel leading to Big Fork Lake, which in turn opened into one of the main lakes of the chain. Four Mile Lake had no other outlet, and thus had no through traffic.

Although tinted slightly brown by tannin, the waters of Four Mile Lake were delightfully transparent, and its shores varied through a rich continuum of plant and animal habitats. The lake did have two inlets. One was a small stream which drained a soggy spruce bog into the northwest bay. The other was Four Mile Creek, a wide flowage choked with cattails and reeds which meandered its way from nearby Spring Lake into the southeast corner. Much of the rest of the shore was high and covered by large white pines.

The land around Four Mile Lake was eventually granted to a homesteader, who built a cabin on Brown's Point.

During the late 1800's, the logging industry moved steadily up the Wisconsin River. By the 1870's, there were seven logging camps in the Three Lakes area. Spruce bogs and cedar swamps, their protective canopies gone, lay open to the drying heat of the summer sun. The torn landscape was often swept by fire. The cry of the mountain lion no longer echoed through the wilderness.

The timber harvesting moved northward, leaving behind a devastated landscape. Once isolated and pristine Four Mile Lake did not escape the woodsman's axe. During the early stages of this logging boom, the homesteader on Four Mile Lake sold the timber on his land to the Woodruff-Maguire Lumber Company, which cut most of the large pines.

One summer day in 1902, an asthmatic old steam launch puffed and coughed through the channel from Big Fork Lake into the waters of Four Mile. Mr. and Mrs. Leo Bishop and their friends Ernest and Ida Wise were on a camping trip, headed for a surviving stand of virgin timber on the distant eastern shore.

Camping in 1902 was not the lightweight affair of nylon and aluminum that it is today. The campers which ventured into the blue waters of Four Mile Lake that sunny day carried heavy iron kettles and skillets, and heavy, bulky canvas tents.

Furthermore, because there was lots of open land and very few people camping for sport, nature enthusiasts of those days knew little of the modern wilderness ethic. The Indians possessed the skills of traceless camping, of course, but few whites saw the need for such measures. These ethics would come some sixty years later to nature enthusiasts as wilderness dwindled and overuse became a serious problem.

In the meantime, sport campers happily honed their skills in the now disappearing art of campcraft. On their arrival at the selected camp site, the Bishops and the Wises busily set to work building a stone fireplace and a rock "icebox" in the lake along shore. They cut tent poles, split logs for a rough-hewn table, dug rain trenches around the tent, and excavated a latrine away from camp, complete with a sanded seat and a screen of freshly-cut hemlock branches! They even cut blocks of sod and hemlock boughs to use as springy mattresses. These heavy handed camping techniques make the sensitive modern backpacker cringe, but it was all very much a part of the wilderness experience in those days.

For several lazy, sunny days the four friends swam in the warm waters of the lake, hiked for hours along intriguing trails, fished from the old steam launch, and cooked delicious fried fish dinners on the stone fireplace.

The Wises enjoyed this trip immensely, and often spoke of it after they had returned to their home in Greenville, Illinois. In the fall of 1903, they decided to again take the train north to Three Lakes, and return to the same camping spot.

Sometime before the shores of Four Mile Lake were logged, the homesteader had moved north to the nearby town of Eagle River. His cabin on Brown's Point was occupied by the only resident of Four Mile Lake, a hermit named Bierbrauer. While the Wises were camping on the lake in 1903, Mr. Bierbrauer approached Ernest Wise and suggested he buy some of the land.

The Wises had fallen deeply in love with Four Mile Lake, and the hermit's words filled them with intense excitement. They lost no time in hiring a one-horse wagon to take them to the homesteader in Eagle River, where they were able to immediately purchase the land. The Wises allowed Bierbrauer to remain on as caretaker, and after a year gave him a piece of the land as a gift.

The rest of the tale of the hermit Bierbrauer is incidental to our story, but is legend in the town of Three Lakes even today. According to a 1949 letter from Ernest Wise to Sam Campbell, "as soon as he (Bierbrauer) received the deed, he sold...(the land), moved down to Planting Ground Lake and returned to his drunken ways, which soon cost him his life." Regional historian Catherine Ralph in The Pine, the Plow, and the Pioneer, a history of Three Lakes, tells how in 1908 a man named "Mr. Beerbower" caught a forty pound fighting muskelunge with his bare hands in Planting Ground Lake. The book also records that circa 1910, this same man was fatally shot on Townline Lake by one Black Mike, in a drunken argument over a woman.

Starting about 1912, the Campbell family began coming up regularly from Chicago to spend their summers near the town of Three Lakes. The campsite in the virgin stand of pines along the eastern shore of Four Mile Lake became their favorite retreat, and they eventually purchased a cabin and some land along the western shore.

When Ernest Wise had bought Lot One on the west bank, he had also acquired the small 1.3 acre island just off shore. Before Long Lake Dam (now Burnt Rollways Dam) was built on the lake chain circa 1910 and raised the water level, this island had actually been part of the mainland, and so was considered part of Lot One. In 1923, the Wises built a cabin, a storehouse, a boathouse, and sunk a well on the island.

When Ernest Wise's health began to deteriorate, the Wises sold their land on Four Mile Lake, including the island, to Sam Campbell in 1937.

When Sam bought the island, he was in his early forties, and was well into his career of animal photography and lecturing. The family's mainland properties also passed to Sam and his brother Don upon the death of the beloved "Dad" Campbell.

Dad Campbell was a kind man with a famous sense of humor. He was often known by the silly nickname "Do-dad," a name Sam invented when he once overheard Ida Cunningham say, "Oh, do, Dad!" The Cunninghams, who regarded the Campbell men as family, grieved with Sam and Don over the loss of their father, and were a great source of comfort.

The Cunningham children were quite grown up by now. They had graduated from the local high school, and Jean and Howard had attended business college in Oshkosh. Beth and Jean still enjoyed spending time at the Sanctuary, but Sam noticed with understanding and amusement that their primary interests were elsewhere. Jean was spending a lot of time with a local young man named Norman Brewster. Beth seemed to be finding a lot in common with Grant Halliday, a young photographer from Chicago who had come up to meet Sam.

The land had changed as well over the ensuing years. Slowly, the northland was beginning to heal itself of the wounds left by the logging era. By the time Sam moved onto the island, the Sanctuary was again a densely wooded paradise, teeming with wildlife. Once again the sense of wilderness prevailed.

Even so, some things would never again be the same. The Native Americans had been displaced from their own country, and their birchbark canoes no longer floated along the shores in the morning mist. The large predators and the moose were gone, too, perhaps never to return. Sam made the small cabin on "Campbell's Island" his summer home, and it became the headquarters for the whole wildlife Sanctuary. A sign hanging over the boathouse proudly proclaimed "The Sanctuary of Wegimind," and indeed, this was the island home which has captured the imagination of so many through the years.

Chapter Eight

Giny

In her heart glows a love for the living and growing things of nature.
　　—*Too Much Salt and Pepper*

"Come on Bobby and Howard," Sam called. "Let's go get some lunch!"

Bobby Kostka and Howard Cunningham looked up as Sam stepped out of the darkroom. They were on the island helping Sam Campbell prepare his latest moving picture, and were learning all the details of film developing, splicing, and editing.

When Sam had moved onto the island, he had converted Ernest Wise's storehouse into his workroom where he prepared his motion pictures.

The boys happily followed Sam out of the workroom. The weather had changed dramatically while they had been inside. Low, gray clouds hung low over the treetops, and a fine, chilly drizzle misted down across the north land. It was good weather for the indoor portion of Sam's work. It was also the kind of weather made for cozy cabins, warm fireplaces and good books, Sam thought as he anticipated the afternoon.

The cabin was only a short distance away from the workroom. As they came in the front door into the family room, the young lady sitting at Sam's semi-circular workdesk looked up with a smile and said, "Well, hello there, you three. Are you giving up for the day?"

"Hello, Dodie," said Sam. "How's your work coming? We decided it's time to take a lunch break. Hungry?"

Sam had employed Dorothy "Dodie" Sheets to help with the burgeoning correspondence of his business. She was another of the young people in the Octagon Club who enjoyed the outdoors and to whom Sam had given the chance to help with his outdoor work.

"Yes, I'm hungry," Dodie declared emphatically. "And I believe you deliberately left that pot of stew on the stove just to torture me all morning!" Everyone knew Sam was a good cook, and the pot of beef stew had been simmering deliciously.

As the four sat down to eat the soup, Dodie looked up with a perfectly straight and businesslike expression on her face. "Oh, by the way Sam, one of your fan letters today is from a young lady living in Chicago who heard one of your lectures last summer. She's the secretary for one of the schools where you showed your film for a lyceum. She was very, what should I say, complimentary, I guess is the word. Her name is Virginia Adams."

Sam looked up from his lunch with a quizzical expression on his face. Dodie's words made him want to laugh, but she didn't seem to be teasing. "OK, sure, I'll look at it later," he said casually.

After lunch, the three young people took their rowboat and headed back to the landing at Four Mile Lake, their work done for the day.

Sam noticed the cabin seemed awfully quiet without them. He had been looking forward to the cozy solitude of the rainy afternoon, but a strange restlessness stirred in his soul. He decided he'd better do some more work, and see if the activity wouldn't cure his restlessness. He sat down at his desk, unsure what work he should do for the rest of the day. He idly picked up the letter from the lady in Chicago and began reading it.

The wind rattled the windows of the cabin, and Sam could still hear water gurgling in the downspout. When he looked out the window at the lake, however, the rain seemed to have stopped.

Sam felt odd. He didn't feel like writing, or like editing his film, or even like curling up in front of the fireplace with a good book. The only cure for such a mood is a good walk, Sam thought. He went down to the boathouse and lowered his favorite canoe into the water.

Sam paddled across the short expanse of lake to the trailhead of Vanishing Lake Trail. As he walked along the trail, fat raindrops hung on the end of the each pine needle, and he was drenched as he brushed against them. He hiked over the low rolling hills, crested the final hill, and saw the tiny jewel of Vanishing Lake nestled in a small valley.

Vanishing Lake is indeed the vanishing remnant of an ancient glacial tarn. Its perimeter is ringed with patiently advancing ranks of sphagnum moss, blueberries, leather leaf, Labrador Tea, swamp laurel, and grotesque carnivorous pitcher plants.

Sam did not descend to the banks of the lake, but sat up on the brow of the hill, watching and musing. After a while, he drew the letter from a pocket and reread it. It surprised Sam that his lecture had made such an impression on the lady. Fan mail was still a novelty for him. The lady seemed to be a real lover of the outdoors. She spoke of her love of animals, hiking and camping, and of her interest in canoeing and learning more about nature.

Sam replaced the letter in his pocket, and sat there thinking. His thoughts soon left the letter, and went on to more familiar topics. His eyes rested on the nearby trees, and he found himself unconsciously ticking off the scientific names of the various species. From where he sat, he identified several types of moss and lichen, and noted the songs of a few birds.

The woods seemed gray and lonely today. That idea bothered Sam, and he attributed his disquieted mood to the rainy low pressure weather system which had advanced over the northlands.

At length, Sam returned to the island. The first thing he did upon entering the cabin was to sit down at his typewriter and write a cordial reply to the letter from the Chicago secretary. Then Sam completely forgot about her. For about ten days.

"Sam!" called Dodie in an unnecessarily loud and insistent tone. "You just got another letter from Virginia Adams!"

Jean and Beth Cunningham were also at the island that day, helping with some of the secretarial duties. At Dodie's call, they perked up with visible interest. "Who is Virginia Adams, Sam?" asked Beth, her eyes twinkling.

Sam looked over at the desk to see Dodie, Jean, Beth, and even Bobby focusing on him with full attention. Sam momentarily felt an uncharacteristic annoyance touch him. He wished his friends would respect his desire to be single. And he had thought of Bobby as an ally!

Sam pushed down the feeling of annoyance, and smiled at his young helpers. "She's just a lady from Chicago who happened to see one of my films."

"Yes, and she wrote to Sam just a few days ago saying how wonderful it was," Dodie added with disarming honesty.

Giny

"You mean this is the second letter you've gotten from her in one week?" Jean asked innocently.

"Two weeks," Sam corrected. The four giggled and glanced at each other. "All right, you nosy little crusaders, I'll tell you one more time. I'm a confirmed bachelor, and that's the way things are going to stay! My life of wandering through the rugged wilderness is definitely not suited for a..." He paused as he noticed the glares of the three girls. "...a family man," he finished weakly. "Now, go play catch with a porcupine and let me alone so I can get some work done!"

The young people laughed as they returned to their work.

Sam elected to reply to this second letter, too, and regular correspondence continued throughout the summer. When the winter lecture season came, Sam was again invited to speak at the high school where Giny Adams worked. In fact, the school sent her to pick him up at the train station, and since neither had eaten, they had lunch together. Sam immediately felt comfortable with her friendship, and marveled at how much he enjoyed the effortless, animated conversation.

She showed up at several more of his Chicago lectures that winter, and Sam grew to enjoy her friendship more and more. They fell quite naturally into the habit of going out together for lunch whenever Sam was in the area. Sam often thought with a touch of amazement that Giny was just as interesting and comfortable a companion as any of his male buddies. In fact, he thought more and more often, she was his most interesting friend.

To Sam's astonishment, he found that Giny, too, had spent several years searching spiritually, and that in 1926 she had joined the same faith which he had recently joined. They had many long and deep discussions about philosophy and spiritual matters. Sam found it remarkable that, even though Giny was obviously as deep a thinker as he, she listened to his ideas carefully and seemed genuinely fascinated by his view of life. He found himself being fascinated by her observations as well, and his own philosophy evolved and grew as it was enriched by her unique perspectives.

Giny visited the Sanctuary in August of 1938. Sam had more fun during that week than he could ever remember. The lakes and sky were a more brilliant blue, the trees were greener, the sunsets more spectacular. Because of the beautiful weather, church met that weekend in a little rustic amphitheater in the forest. Never could Sam remember a more meaningful service.

Sam surrounded himself and Giny with his local friends while she was in town, and all were immediately drawn to her. Giny had a warmth which put others at ease, and despite their age differences, Jean and Beth and she felt at once like old friends.

During all the hiking, swimming, canoeing, campfire suppers, and other activities of the week, Sam's friends couldn't help notice with interest that Sam wasn't paying as much attention to them as usual. He was friendly, of course, but usually Sam was completely absorbed with the person to whom he was speaking; it was one of the traits which drew people to him like a magnet.

When Giny was around, however, Sam was focused on one person—Giny. The two of them constantly joked and traded hilarious insults back and forth. Even when they were talking with other members of the group, their attention seemed to be fixed squarely on each other.

Sam was probably the only one who didn't quite get what was going on. He plunged with happy abandon into the days of fun, still blissfully ignorant of the tremendous awakening in his soul which would change his life forever. He as yet had no inkling that his former satisfaction in the bachelor's life was gone, never to be recaptured. He naively believed things would go on just as before when the happy week was done. Another wonderful friend, more precious memories, at parting a cheerful anticipation of next time.

Good times pass quickly. The glorious week was careening headlong to a close as Giny and Sam drove slowly along the forest lane toward town, laughing over some silly joke until the tears spilled down their faces. The light of the morning sun cast the lakes in warm golden hues. The warm summer air brushed their faces through the open windows.

Sam found himself standing with Giny on the platform of the train station in Three Lakes as the old steam engine hissed to a stop. Just time to laugh a little more, load the bags, and see Giny up the stairs. The air was thick with enthusiastic thank you's and good-bye's through the open coach window. The ancient engine laboriously picked up speed, and he finally lost sight of her smiling face and waving hand.

The realization was slowly dawning upon Sam that Giny was no ordinary friend. She was a person without equal, a person whose presence he felt he could not do without.

Sam was by nature a trusting person, but he felt a more complete and deeper trust in this woman than he had ever felt in his life. He felt no shame at crying in front of her when he was in pain, he sensed no need to hide from her the defects of his character, he never felt a need to impress her nor the pressure to be someone he was not. Her openness and warmth, her acceptance and respect, brought an unparalleled peace to Sam's heart.

She sensed his every mood; even at a distance she seemed to instinctively know when he was having a difficult time. Sam felt there must be some kind of mystical connection between them. He thought of her every moment of every day. Even when his work demanded his undivided attention, she was there, a warm presence standing at the back of his thoughts.

For the life of him, Sam could no longer summon up the rugged individualistic pride he had taken so long in his bachelor state. His determined pursuit of self reliance seemed outdated and irrelevant as he instinctively leaned on Giny for emotional support.

This presented a problem. On the one hand, he was no longer satisfied with being alone. On the other, he knew without a doubt there was only one person who could ever complete the hollow which had appeared in his soul. There was only one solution.

Samuel A. Campbell and Virginia M. Adams were married on June 10 of 1941. They had an outdoor wedding in Lucile's garden; Sam, of course, was dressed in his trade mark northwoods shirt, breeches, and high leather boots! Even as they said their vows, Sam still could not believe his good fortune nor stop thanking God. The fact that Giny was as eager to be with him forever as he was to be with her seemed an unbelievably wonderful dream, and he was afraid he might awaken at any moment. How could life be so good to him?

Chapter Nine

Sanctuary of Wegimind

Soft silence, strong faith, restful patience, and peace of mind reign when we dwell in blessed sylvan mansions.
—*Nature's Messages*

The call of the whippoorwill marked the end of the sunset hour. The lake was calm, caught in the vaporous enchantment of the moment. Gathering storm clouds filtered out the golden colors of the westering sun, spreading a bronze sheen over the waters. Across the lake, two islands lay like ships at anchor in the rising mists. On the larger of the two sits the cabin home of the late Sam Campbell, noted naturalist, philosopher, author and lecturer. Sam named the western tip of the island "Sunset Point." Here was a log bench where he and his guests could enjoy the beauty of the North Country and nature; his only desire was to share it with all men. His philosophy was rich with inspiration and love for all life, human as well as non-human.

I let the canoe drift into the beauty of the moment; the ramparts of the stump-filled bay, aglow with old rose and magenta, stood boldly against the skyline; fish splashed, swallows dived and dipped, a loon called, and finally, as the twilight deepened, the call of a whippoorwill echoed across the hills.

— *Walt Goldsworthy in*
Wilderness Reflections

It had been Giny's idea to honeymoon in the Quetico. No destination could have appealed more to Sam, of course, but he had never thought to find a female companion who relished wilderness as much as he. In fact, Giny had dispelled most of his misconceptions concerning women. She possessed a rugged endurance for the trail, easily handled a paddle, skillfully swung snowshoes, and took in all of nature's adventures cheerfully and enthusiastically, without complaint of discomfort.

Sam and Giny returned from their honeymoon in the Canadian Shield to the cozy little cabin on the island in Four Mile Lake. Sam had spent the spring and early summer before the wedding adding a bedroom, bathroom, and indoor plumbing to the cabin. All of his hard work met with Giny's enthusiastic approval.

The island was really the top of a little hill which had at one time been joined to the mainland by a marshy peninsula. The locals said that in those days one could walk right across during dry weather.

When the gates of the dam on Long Lake swung shut circa 1910, the level of Four Mile Lake rose ten inches, isolating the hillock from the mainland. The banks of the little island rose up steeply to the higher ground in the middle, which was fairly flat except for a swampy depression near the north shore.

The cabin perched on high ground near the south bank. There were so many windows in the main room that Sam said there was "hardly enough wood to hold up the roof." These huge windows along the south wall afforded an expansive, wide angle view of the main body of the lake and the dusky fringes of its far shores. A large fireplace and mantle flanked by bookcases lined the east wall, and Sam's big semi-circular wooden writing desk occupied the southeast corner. Across the room, under more large windows, stood a small wooden, oval dining table and two hand-carved wooden chairs. The whole inside of the cabin was finished in the beautiful golden-yellow wood of pine.

Sitting in this room while eating a meal, reading, studying, or merely lounging beside the roaring fireplace, one felt an integral part of the forest scene outside. Vivid blues and greens and golds washed into the room on bright summer days; and the black angry clouds, winds and rains, thrashing trees and heaving lake marched through the room on stormy days.

The Sanctuary saw many happy events that summer. Early in the spring, before any of the Campbells had arrived from Chicago, both Cunningham girls had said their marriage vows at the little outdoor chapel in the forest behind Campbells' mainland cabin. They had planned a double ceremony, but Norman's leave time from the service had come a week earlier than expected. One cold rainy day, the launch carrying Jean, Norm, and the wedding party steamed through the drizzle, past the remnants of melting ice floes, into Four Mile Lake. The Sanctuary, happy to be involved, threw rice after the vows—in the form of a snow shower!

Beth and Grant were married at the same outdoor chapel a week later. Once again the Sanctuary got into the act; it deluged the party with a pouring rain right after the vows were taken! The ceremony was held before a small group of relatives; undaunted, they simply went into the cabin and all dressed up in old, but dry, clothes!

By the time Sam and Giny returned from their honeymoon, Norm was back in the service, and Beth and Grant had moved down to Chicago. Grant would enter the military at a later time.

Now, even as Sam and Giny cherished their new life together, their thoughts were never far from the war in Europe. Bobby Kostka, Norm Brewster and the Olson boys had all been called to serve, along with many other of Sam and Giny's younger friends. America was readying for war.

Pearl Harbor was attacked at 7:55 a.m. on December 7, and the United States was plunged into World War II.

Sam's books and lectures often had a patriotic flavor during the war years. While he made it clear that philosophically he considered the war a morally just and righteous cause, he also wrote passages which wrestled with the realities of young people having to kill other young people just like themselves, neither one hating the other. He wrote, "I cannot justify war...I only know that at times it is the lesser of two evils—the loss of freedom being the greater."

For Sam, another major event of 1941 was the publication of the first book of his Forest Life Series. *How's Inky* rolled off the presses at Bobbs-Merrill Publishing Company in time to be incorporated into Sam's lecture tours that fall. *How's Inky* told the tale of Sam's bachelor days, when Inky the porcupine was a baby and Bobby "North" Kostka and "Judge" Tom Norton were visiting the island. It was the major debut of Sam's trademark writing style of combining nature stories with interpretive philosophy.

The years between 1941 and 1962 span the period of Sam Campbell's life for which he is best known. He and Giny spent part of most summers traveling, gathering film and book material, and spent the balance of the warm months at their island home writing a new book and preparing the lectures and films for the coming season.

When the leaves fell and the snows came, they would move back to their home at 220 Oak Knoll Road in Barrington, Illinois, which they used as a base for their winter lecture travels. In all, Sam produced over 150,000 feet of film and conducted over 9,000 lectures during his 30 plus year career. He was featured on radio and television shows; Midwestern listeners loved to tune in to his program "The Sanctuary Hour." He was of course a much sought after speaker at schools. In the later years, he and Giny led tours all over the world under the auspices of their company, The Sam Campbell Tours and Nature Lectures.

The flavor, and many facts, of these years are well-chronicled in the twelve Forest Life Series storybooks.

Jean and Norm Brewster, and Beth and Grant Halliday settled in Three Lakes after the war. Bobby Kostka married and traveled around the world leading tours. He said he had gotten "sand in his shoes" while traveling with Sam, and had "never been able to get it out."

Sam, once emphatically self characterized as a "dyed-in-the-wool bachelor," now said meeting Giny was "the grandest thing that ever happened to me." Sam's bachelor ways didn't disappear at once, however. Giny told the Cunningham family how she had tried to get Sam to pick up his clothes and put them away so they wouldn't wrinkle. Sam declared, "No, I won't put them away! Who cares if they're wrinkled?" and so saying, he threw them on the floor and jumped up and down on them. Sam and Giny both seemed to find the incident hilarious.

Sam belonged to the prestigious Lake Shore Club on Lake Shore Drive in Chicago, but for many years he couldn't go up to eat in the dining room because he refused to dress in the proper attire. Giny must have had some success over the years, however, because Bobby Kostka later told the story of how he had met the Campbells at a restaurant in Chicago, and was shocked to find Sam wearing a tie.

Bobby didn't like to see the changes in Sam, and he walked right up without a word, snatched off the tie, and tossed it out the open window to the street below!

During these years, the tourist industry expanded rapidly in the Three Lakes area, and the lake shores became dotted with cabins.

About 1947, Carl Marty, Jr. built the Northernaire, a modern resort hotel, on Deer Lake. Many of the famous and wealthy came to the Northernaire for summer and winter sports and entertainment. Mr. Marty was also widely known for his love of animals. He had pet deer, raccoons, porcupines, skunks and bear which roamed the grounds of the resort. He and Sam grew to be great friends, and the Campbells sometimes stayed at the hotel on winter visits to the Sanctuary.

Sam Campbell had actually promoted tourism in the region, but he felt many conflicting emotions as he saw the wilderness disappear. To be sure, the Nicolet National Forest shielded the land to the east, and the Three Lakes area itself was still richly wooded and had abundant wildlife, but the remoteness of the northwoods had receded.

Sam's conservationist convictions grew deeper as he saw wilderness rapidly disappearing all over the country. He joined Sig Olson in the efforts to protect the canoe country from development, and to ban motors and pontoon planes from the remote lakes. The efforts of many resulted at last in the designation of a paddle-only wilderness area called Boundary Waters Canoe Area Wilderness. The Boundary Waters Canoe Area Wildness Act (Public Law 95–495), passed in October of 1978, gave full wilderness protection to this area.

Chapter Ten

Just a Beginning

*THE END
which is always
just a beginning*
—*Fiddlesticks and Freckles*

It was March 28, 1962. As John Walter Goldsworthy and his friend Edward Boehm, president of the Three Lakes Chamber of Commerce, drove along the north country roads toward Three Lakes, Walt's mind drifted back to the day he had first met Sam Campbell.

Walt and his brother Vernon had moved to Three Lakes in 1946 and founded the Thunder Lake Cranberry Company, which cultivated cranberries in the bogs around Thunder Lake. Walt had heard of Campbell and, like many of the people of Three Lakes, had thought his positions on conservation and hunting a bit silly and radical.

The younger Goldsworthy was a civic-minded man, and was becoming an active member of the community. One night at a Rotary Club supper in the basement of the Union Congregational Church, Walt had met Sam face to face.

Walt remembered the warmth and friendship radiating from the man, and how Sam grasped his hand and focused all his attention on Walt as though Walt were the most important person in the room.

Over the years, Walt had learned to admire Sam Campbell and the ideals for which he stood. Sam had become something of a role model and mentor for Walt, as well as a valued friend.

Later, Walt had become the first interpretive forest naturalist ever hired by U. S. Forest Service. He lived with his wife Doris and their young children in a log cabin up at Franklin Lake in Nicolet National Forest. As his understanding of nature reached greater depths, he himself became an ardent conservationist and environmentalist. His writing career also developed as he wrote the 22-year newspaper column "Lakes and Woods," and a book of philosophical nature essays called *Wilderness Reflections*. Through the years, Walt had became one of Sam's greatest supporters.

Walt's thoughts moved back to the present as they neared the town of Rhinelander. They were almost home. He and Ed were driving back to Three Lakes after transacting some business in Chicago. While there, they had visited Sam and Giny Campbell in their winter home at 220 Oak Knoll Road in Barrington, Illinois. The two Three Lakes men had stopped by to visit and to tell Sam about plans for a testimonial dinner the town was planning in his honor on July 29.

Goldsworthy later wrote in his Three Lakes News column "Lakes and Woods,"

"As Sam read the many letters from the great and small across the nation, I noticed tears cornered in his eyes as he expressed his appreciation for the kindness and thoughtfulness of 'all those good folks,' as Sam expressed it."

"When Ed Boehm told him of the community-wide support being given the testimonial dinner, Sam was deeply moved...'I didn't realize,' he said, 'that I had so many friends in Three Lakes. This makes me very happy, for Three Lakes is very dear to Ginny (sic) and me and I hope I can do much for it in the years ahead. God willing, I will!'"

Walt and Ed had said their goodbyes and Sam had walked them to their car, saying, "Have a safe journey home, fellows; give our best regards to all the folks in Three Lakes."

As they finally pulled into the town of Three Lakes, Walt turned to Ed Boehm suddenly. "You know, Ed, Sam Campbell didn't look all that well to me. He didn't seem quite like himself. What did you think?"

Ed frowned slightly. "I had the same feeling. He didn't seem to feel all that well. He was as cheerful as ever, but he didn't seem to have all that energy which I associate with him. I suppose all that traveling around the world and such could tire a person out. He did say he was really looking forward to getting some serious northwoods rest and quiet."

Walt nodded. "He needs to get away from that city!"

"Sam! What's wrong? You look like you feel terrible," worried Giny as she entered the living room.

It was Wednesday, April 11. The Campbells were still at their home in Barrington, for Sam had a few more lectures to give that season. They were looking forward to the soon-coming day, however, when they would wrap up the lecture work and head for the peace of the Sanctuary.

Sam had been having chest pains off and on for several weeks. Now, he sagged down onto the couch with a moan. His skin was gray and he was gasping for breath.

"You just can't go on your lecture tour this weekend, Sam. You're not well at all. I'm terribly worried." Giny knelt beside him and stroked his head, unsure what to do. She wasn't used to seeing her strong, energetic, cheerful husband immobilized by pain, unable even to talk.

In a few moments, Sam seemed to feel a bit better. "You're right, Giny. I can't go this weekend. Would you mind calling Norman Hallock and asking him to take my Sunday lecture? His phone number is on my desk."

Norman Hallock of Hendersonville, North Carolina, owned Hallock Travelogues and was Sam's colleague in nature films and lectures. They had been friends for twenty-five years, and they filled in for one another in emergencies.

Norman Hallock agreed to give Sam's Sunday lecture, and Giny went back into the living room to check on her husband.

On Friday, April 13, 1962, as Norman Hallock made preparations for the weekend tour, he received a phone call from Giny Campbell. Sam Campbell had died of a massive heart attack just a few hours earlier.

Listen, and I shall tell you a secret. We shall not all die, but suddenly, in the twinkling of an eye, every one of us will be changed as the trumpet sounds! The trumpet will sound and the dead shall be raised beyond the reach of corruption, and we who are alive shall suddenly be utterly changed. For this perishable nature of ours must be wrapped in imperishability; these bodies which are mortal must be wrapped in immortality. So when the perishable is lost in the imperishable, the mortal lost in the immortal, this saying will come true:

Death is swallowed up in victory.

For where now, O death, is your power to hurt us? Where now, O grave, is the victory you hoped to win?...All thanks to God, then, who gives us the victory over these things through our Lord Jesus Christ!

—I Corinthians 15:51–55,57
Phillips translation

Afterword

I have journeyed back over many years in support of this account of the life and work of Sam Campbell; and this has served to draw up out of those years a renewed appreciation for people, places and times until now partly forgotten.

That his work is timeless and his philosophy as much needed now as then is witnessed by second and third generation readers who write or still come to the north country in search of traces of Vanishing Lake, Sanctuary Lake, and all the people and wildlife friends that make up the Sam Campbell legacy of books.

Several of the characters in his books are composites of my childhood family. Thus, as one blessed in knowing much of the background of his writing, I feel it important to say to those who take up this quest:

Sam's writing is ageless, but if we locate each character and place, see them as aged, changed or gone, then the books become aged and limited too.

Enjoy your visits, your delving into the past where you can. But Sam's purpose was not to map out a place in Wisconsin where HE lived and worked...but rather to map out a place in each reader's heart where THEY can find the same peace and joy that he did. YOUR Sanctuary Lake is somewhere in the best of your living and thinking, and you will know it when you find it.

                Jean Cunningham Brewster
                Three Lakes, Wisconsin

Appendix

Chapter One

Most of Chapter One was written by Michael J. Battistone, who was a medical student at Duke University while the author was a graduate student there. Chapter One is reproduced here by Dr. Battistone's permission.

Sam Campbell talked about the Voices of the Woods several times in his books. In *Too Much Salt and Pepper*, Carol, a girl visiting the Sanctuary, hears the Voices when she learns how to listen. In *The Seven Secrets of Somewhere Lake*, the adolescent Hi-Bub manages to tune out the confusing voices of war and false values, and again hears the Voices of the Woods. Sig Olson mentioned the Voices in his book *The Singing Wilderness*. Sam Campbell told in *Nature's Messages* of first hearing the Voices of the Woods as a boy camping along a river. The camping trip in Chapter One is based on his description of this event. The specific choice of the Iroquois River and the exact details of the camping trip are based on speculation by author Michael J. Battistone.

Sam Campbell wrote about visiting his grandfather's farm and playing with the dog Sport in *Eeny, Meeny, Miney, Mo—and Still-Mo*. The experience with the flock of geese and the account of Sam's school days appeared in articles in the June 19, 1962 edition of The Three Lakes News. Young Sam's interest in the Voyageurs and the Canadian canoe country is taken from *A Tippy Canoe and Canada Too*.

Chapter One

Watseka is a small Illinois town about 80 miles south of Chicago near the Indiana border. The information on the Lyman family history came from the following sources (see Bibliography for complete book references):

Portrait and Biographical Record of Iroquois County, Illinois, pp. 414–415.
Obituary of Andrew J. Lyman, Watseka Republican, March 12, 1912.
Receipt by heirs of Andrew J. Lyman.
Obituary of John Thomas Lyman, Watseka Republican, September 11, 1949.
1880 census, Martinton Township, Andrew J. Lyman.

These materials were provided by Grace Bowen of the Iroquois County Genealogical Society in Watseka.

Lyman Family Tree:

A.   JOHN LYMAN
(Emigrated from Germany)

A-1.   JOHN LYMAN, JR.
(m. Sarah Baum)

A-2.   JONATHON LYMAN
(m. Sarah Baum after death of John Lyman, Jr.)

A-1-1. ANDREW JACKSON LYMAN
(m. Elmira Brandenburg; had a farm in Watseka)

A-1-1-1. MARY C. LYMAN

A-1-1-2. KATHERINE (Kittie) CAMPBELL
(m. Arthur James Campbell)

A-1-1-3. IDA P. BEAN

A-1-1-4. JOHN THOMAS (Tom) LYMAN
(m. Elsie DeWitt, d. 1905; m. Minnie Leeder, d.1937)

A-1-1-5. FRANK LYMAN
(died young)

A-1-1-6. CORA SHAW
(m. S. P. Shaw)

A-1-1-7. ALTA SMALL

A-1-1-2-1. DON CAMPBELL

A-1-1-2-2. SAMUEL ARTHUR CAMPBELL
(m. Virginia Adams)

A-1-1-2-3. LUCILE (Lucille?)
(Sam's "adopted sister"; same as cousin Lucile Gordon?)

A-1-1-4-1. LUCILE GORDON

----END----

Appendix

Chapter Two

Three Lakes historian Walt Goldsworthy stated in a letter to the author that "Four Mile" is the original spelling and "Fourmile" a more modern spelling. He humorously added that those ignorant of the past tend to alter the future, "such as the camper who came into Franklin Lake telling of seeing a bear by "NINEEMILEE" Creek!" Sam Campbell used the spelling "Four Mile" in his books.

Sam Campbell's description of his first visit to the Three Lakes area in 1909 is quoted in the June 19, 1962 edition of The Three Lakes News. The origin of the word "Wegimind" is explained in many of Sam Campbell's writings, for example in the introduction to *Nature's Messages*.

The Campbells' favorite camping spot on the east shore of Four Mile Lake is further described in Chapter Seven and its appendix. Information on the Sloans came from conversations with Jean Brewster of Three Lakes.

The story in Chapter Two of Sam shooting a deer is true to life. Jean Brewster remembers Sam Campbell describing how his mother had told him that someday he would no longer wish to hunt. In *Too Much Salt and Pepper*, Sam told Carol "I never saw the native friendship of so-called wild animals when I was a killer of them." Sam wrote several times of his mother's attitude toward wildlife. According to the headline article in the June 19, 1962 edition of The Three Lakes News, "(Sam's) father...Arthur James Campbell (was) a sportsman and nature lover. His mother, Katherine Lyman

Campbell was a deep student of nature. She wrote many poems and articles on the living world, and raised Sam with the understanding that he had an obligation to love and protect all things that live. His parents took Sam into nature by way of hikes and camping trips, teaching him in identify plants and animals."

Sam quoted his mother in *The Conquest of Grief* as saying to him, "Conduct your life as though you were the model after which all mankind is sculptured."

Sam Campbell wrote in *Moose Country* that as a boy he became literally sick with longing for wild, unspoiled places. He mentioned in *The Conquest of Grief* that his brother Don was a more practical person.

Jean Brewster recalled that as a young man, Sam Campbell stayed home writing while his brother Don and his father worked at Sloan Valve Company in Chicago. The 1963 edition of *Who's Who* and the Three Lakes News article mentioned above records Sam's university attendance and his jobs as real estate salesman and music teacher. A letter from Giny Campbell to Judy Hanson (see "Miscellany") mentions the exact instruments Sam taught.

Sam described in *The Conquest of Grief* how his mother selflessly used up her strength helping others. Conversations with Jean Brewster and others have revealed Sam's early antipathy toward the idea of marriage.

There is some confusion concerning the date of Kittie Campbell's death. *The Conquest of Grief* first gives the date as June, 1929, then later as June 17, 1927. Jean Brewster believes the latter date to be correct.

The evening of the day his mother passed away, Sam Campbell wrote "What indescribable horror swept over me as the doctor pronounced this final judgment!

Chapter Two

Bitterness, rebellion, hopelessness, and morbid plans flooded my thoughts. Intolerable glimpses of the empty future flashed across my mind...It seemed the end of happiness, reason, ambition, plans-everything!" *(The Conquest of Grief)* The author surmises from this that Sam may have contemplated suicide. The exact details of his location and actions at that time are speculative, however.

Appendix

Chapter Three

In *The Conquest of Grief*, Sam Campbell wrote "My father and I were returning to the city, after having purchased a lot in a quiet little country cemetery. So immune had we felt to calamity that this provision had not been made. We were silent, almost sullen, in our inward battle against grief and bitterness." He then went on to describe the spiritual encounter experienced by him and his father, and also by his brother, sister, and cousin. The anecdote of the dog Count comes from *Eeny, Meeny, Miney, Mo—and Still-Mo*.

Sam Campbell described in *The Conquest of Grief* the reflective months following his mother's death.

Appendix

Chapter Four

An article in the June 19, 1962 edition of *The Three Lakes News* quoted Sam Campbell: "There was a divided opinion even among experts as to what should and should not be done in this field (of conservation)—and opinion was constantly changing. Then one day as I paddled my canoe along the shores of Four Mile Lake, the matter was made clear to me. I had been discouraged with militant conservation, and shocked too, at public indifference on nature matters. But I saw clearly that in this latter situation whatever talents I had as a photographer, lecturer and writer, would find their best field in seeking to awaken nature appreciation."

The same article notes that "The real break in Sam's career came when he found he had exceptional talent for the lecture platform. About 1929 he made his first films of animal life, and presented them to the public. The central theme of his talks was conservation and immediately there was widespread demand for his services. The Chicago and Northwestern Railway discovered him, and made him their official lecturer—a position he held for 22 years."

The geography of Four Mile Lake as described in the chapter comes from the author's own experiences there. The description of Sam Campbell's typical dress was compiled from conversations with those who knew him, notably Jean Brewster and Art Meyers of Three Lakes. The narration for the film is a compilation of quotes from several of Sam Campbell's books and from his taped narration of his film *Come to the North Country*.

This was the last film he produced, and the only one which had a sound tract.

The "half-joking" rumor that Sam provided cotton for the mice in his cabin to use for nests was recounted by his neighbor, the late Mrs. Doris Brandt Koller of Spring Lake.

Appendix

Chapter Five

This Chapter is based on Jean Brewster's memories of how Sam Campbell met her family. She supplied descriptions and history of the Thunder Lake Store, and detailed the route Sam Campbell traveled to get there. The Brewsters also mentioned that Sam usually drove a Buick.

Roy and Ida Cunningham were Jean Brewster's parents, and Beth and Howard her siblings. This family was known to Sam Campbell's readers as "Ada, Ray and June." June, the beautiful, dark haired girl in the books, was a composite character based on Jean and Beth Cunningham.

John Shabodock was indeed a Potawatomi chief who lived in a cabin back in the woods near the Three Lakes area (see *The Pine, the Plow, and the Pioneer*). "Big John Shawano," the local Indian chief who hitched a ride with Sam, Giny, Bob, Marge, and Hi-Bub one Christmas (*On Wings of Cheer*) may have actually been Chief John Shabodock.

The story of the wolverine and the Indian named Ben who lived in a cabin on the north shore of Four Mile Lake can be found in *Fiddlesticks and Freckles*. The clearing where Ben's cabin stood and where the Meadows family of *Fiddlesticks and Freckles* camped and docked their boat is still there. The author has had the pleasure of camping in that very spot.

Sam Campbell often hosted campfire suppers, and Jean Brewster supplied a description of the food and music. The words to "A-rolling My Ball" came from Grace Lee Nute's *The Voyageur's Highway*, which also gives the music and an English translation for curious readers. The words and music to "At the Clear Flowing Fountain," another Voyageur song mentioned by Sam in *Moose Country*, can also be found in Grace Lee Nute's book. "When You Come to the End of a Perfect Day" by Carrie Jacobs Bond was the song that Bob, Marge, and Hi-Bub sang as they crouched under their overturned canoe during a storm in canoe country (*Moose Country*).

The conversation around the campfire is based on the author's interpretation of some of Sam Campbell's philosophy.

Sam Campbell became a leader in Cunninghams' home church. He later taught Sunday School, and was instrumental in building the beautiful new church which stands in Eagle River today.

Appendix

Chapter Six

The essay "Higher Finance" in *Nature's Messages* tells how during the Depression Sam Campbell spent his last few dollars on a trip to the north country. He called it one of the best investments he ever made.

Bobby Kostka, a young man from Cicero, Illinois known in the books as "Bobby North," did travel to canoe country with Sam Campbell on at least one occasion (see Sig Olson's remarks in the appendix for Chapter Ten). Jean Brewster and Dorothy Hoelter supplied information on Bobby Kostka and the Octagon Club.

The route from Three Lakes to Ely is based on the one Jean Brewster's family used to take. She described "the long, winding road to Ely," and told how as children they would get car sick and have to walk for a while. Sam's comparison of the road to a "great serpent" can be found in *Moose Country*.

Jim Pascoe, a well-known outfitter in Ely, wrote to the author in a letter dated January 26, 1989: "Border Lakes Outfitting has been sold to the U. S. Forest Service, under the Wilderness Bill. The business will no longer function and the government will revert the property back to its natural state. Border Lakes was a very historical and prestigious company, starting business in 1929...Sam Campbell did make some canoe trips in this area in the years gone by. He made some with Sig Olson, who was an owner of Border Lakes Outfitting...One trip in particular went to Kawnipiminacock*. Days gone forever." Elizabeth Olson also tells of the days when she and Sig were part owners of Border Lakes.

The two Olson boys Sig, Jr., and Bob were incorporated into the character "Sandy" in Sam Campbell's books. Sig, Jr., who now lives in Alaska, has fond memories of those days. John Sanstead was a guide for Border Lakes Outfitting. He wrote from his home in Winton, Minnesota, in a letter postmarked February 6, 1989, that he "went with (Sam) and Sig as a guide between 50 to 60 years ago."

Elizabeth Olson and many others have mentioned to the writer that Sam Campbell always took his guitar along wherever he went. For the amusing story of how a light-traveling Indian guide reacted to Sam's bulky guitar in canoe country, the reader is directed to *A Tippy Canoe and Canada Too*.

The story of the disappearing canoes of Basswood Lake was actually a personal experience of Doug Jordan, an Ely outfitter. Jordan recounted the story to the author. Norman Hallock of Hallock Travelogues remembers the film segment of Sam Campbell dancing with his canoe; and Sam Campbell told the beaver story ("The Sweetest Story Ever Told") to Carol in the book *Too Much Salt and Pepper*.

Beyond these facts, the exact date and details of the drive north and the canoe route are fictional.

* The lake to which Sam Campbell referred in his books as "Kahnipi" is now labeled "Kawnipi" on most maps. Jean Brewster has an old map with the spelling Kahnipiminanikok, which is the spelling used in this chapter. Doug Jordan (an Ely outfitter) and John Sanstead give the old spelling as Kawnipiminacock.

Appendix

Chapter Seven

The Three Lakes history in this chapter was condensed from *The Pine, the Plow, and the Pioneer* and conversations with Walt Goldsworthy and Jean Brewster. The history of Four Mile Lake was compiled from documents and information supplied by the late Ralph Leatzow (see "Miscellany"). Mr. Leatzow was a friend of Sam Campbell's. He bought the island property from Giny several years after Sam's death. He was a most helpful and gracious host when the author visited the island while researching this book.

Sam Campbell kept the documents which proved the island was part of Lot One. When Ralph Leatzow bought the island, Giny Campbell left him this packet of documents, including the following:

Island No. One, Four Mile Lake

In 1902, Mr. and Mrs. Leo Bishop took Ernest and Ida Wise by steam launch, for a camping trip on Four Mile Lake, at the camping place in the virgin timber on the east shore. This campsite later became a favorite of the Campbell family.

While the Bishops and the Wises were in this camp, the shore line of Lot No. Two and Island No. One were swept by a forest fire.

In the fall of 1903 Mr. and Mrs. Wise were camped on Lot Ten on Four Mile Lake, fell in love with the lake and its surroundings and arranged to purchase Lots One, Two, and Ten.

The patent from the U. S. Government and the deed for purchase were recorded in 1904. Ernest Wise paid first taxes in January, 1905. The Woodruff-Maguire

Lumber Company had purchased from the homesteader and cut the most of the merchantable timber from the land, including the larger pine trees on Island No. One, probably supposing same to be a part of Lot One.

On account of the fire of 1902, there were many dead trees on the island. Mr. Wise had these cut in 1911, cut into sections and laid in a marshy place in the center of the island.

In 1909, Attorney Neal Brown, of Wausau, gave opinion that as Island No. One was within the lines of Lot One and in shallow water, that Island No. One was a part of Lot One. In 1911, the County Surveyor, Mr. D. H. Vaughn, surveyed on the ice and made a plat—on record at Rhinelander, declared Island No. One to be not an island before Long Lake Dam was built, therefore is a part of Lot One.

Neither of above suggested that the U. S. Government or the State of Wisconsin might hold a title to Island No. One, but Surveyor Vaughn did state that the small island No. Two did not belong to the mainland on account of distance and navigable water.

Mr. Wise, ignorant of the title the State of Wisconsin might have in Island No. One, in 1923 had built a cottage, storehouse and small boat storehouse and had a well dug and driven between rocks.

In 1926, Henry Gagen, assessor, made affidavit for the seven years beginning 1919, he had assessed this island as part of Lot One and Mr. Wise had paid taxes on same. The Three Lakes assessor's and collector books show that taxes have been paid on the improvements beginning with 1923, and on Lot No. One beginning with 1905.

On account of failing health Mr. Wise sold island and improvements to Mr. Sam Campbell and the deed was recorded last April 1939, after the 1938 taxes were paid.

Appendix

Chapter Eight

The author found little information on Giny Campbell's background or courtship. Betty Lamon of Three Lakes believes that Giny originally came from New York, although she met Sam in Chicago. Some have suggested she has a brother, Billy Adams, who may live in Connecticut or Florida.

Walt Goldsworthy recalls that Giny was working as a secretary for a high school principal in Chicago when she met Sam. He also notes that Giny was a "city gal," and that there was a big difference between her and Sam's personalities. Sam was a dreamer; Giny was an astute business woman who turned Sam's talents into a goldmine.

In conversations, Jean Brewster has pointed out that while in Chicago, Giny joined the same denomination Sam later joined. She believes they may have first met through church youth groups. According to church records, Giny joined the Church of Christ, Scientist on November 5, 1926, while living in Chicago. Sam joined in June of 1931. At that time, his address was 739 William St., River Forest, Illinois.

According to a letter to the author from Dorothy "Dodie" J. Sheets (later Dorothy Hoelter), she (Dodie) worked as Sam Campbell's secretary, and in fact remembers when the first letter came from Giny Adams: "She (Giny) had heard him lecture on the North Woods and wrote to thank him; their romance continued from that point."

As Jean Brewster has pointed out, although Dorothy Sheets did visit the Sanctuary, she was from the River Forest, Illinois area, and worked for Sam there. In this Chapter, I have taken license to move the action up to Three Lakes. The presence of Bobby Kostka and Howard Cunningham in this chapter is true-to-life, but fictional. The two boys were much alike, and were good friends.

Sam Campbell did convert Ernest Wise's storehouse into a workroom, Giny did visit for a week at the Sanctuary (see photo section), and the Campbells were married June 10, 1941. The place and details of the wedding are taken from a letter from Giny to Judy Hanson (see "Miscellany").

These are the facts. The rest of Chapter Eight is speculative.

Appendix

Chapter Nine

Sam Campbell wrote in *A Tippy Canoe and Canada Too* that he and Giny had spent their honeymoon in the Canadian canoe country. The author only surmises that this was Giny Campbell's suggestion.

Jean and Norman Brewster supplied the account of their wedding at the Sanctuary. They also mentioned that Sam was remodeling the cabin that spring. The details of the remodeling came from Ralph Leatzow, the friend of Sam Campbell's who owned the cabin when I visited. Ralph Leatzow also showed me the documents which prove the island was once a part of the mainland.

Sam Campbell described the many windows in the cabin on the soundtrack to his film *Come to the North Country*. The description of the island and the cabin come from the author's own visit there, and from Jean Brewster's pictures of the inside of the cabin.

Sam Campbell talked about the war to Hi-Bub in *The Seven Secrets of Somewhere Lake*.

According to the 1963 edition of *Who's Who*, Sam Campbell "produced 150,000 feet of nature films to illustrate lectures", and gave "9,000 lectures in 30 years."

Woodland Portraits, a compilation of essays from *Nature's Messages* which was published posthumously, states that "he appeared many times on radio and television; his program, 'The Sanctuary Hour,' was a favorite in the Midwest."

Jean Brewster remembers that Sam called himself a "dyed-in-the-wool bachelor" who planned never to marry. The June 19, 1962 edition of the Three Lakes News quotes Sam as writing that his marriage to Virginia Adams was "the grandest thing that ever happened" to him.

Jean Brewster also recounted the stories about Sam jumping on his clothes, about Bobby Kostka and Sam's tie, and about Bobby Kostka's later tours and the "sand" in his shoes.

The Northernaire is a graceful building which still stands on Deer Lake. This is the "modern hotel" where Sam tried those disastrous snow skiing lessons in the book *Moose Country*. In the Museum at Three Lakes hangs a portrait of Carl Marty surrounded by his pet animals. These are the "baby animals" Sam Campbell wrote of in the beginning chapters of *The Seven Secrets of Somewhere Lake*. Readers will note that Seven Secrets was dedicated to Carl Marty.

In *Moose Country*, Sam Campbell wrote of the intrusion of motors and planes into the canoe country wilderness. He greatly respected Sig Olson's efforts to preserve that country, and dedicated *Moose Country* to him. Boundary Waters lies in Superior National Forest on the U.S. side of the Minnesota border. Quetico Provincial Park lies in Ontario on the Canadian side of the border. What Sam Campbell referred to as "canoe country" now comprises this international wilderness area.

Appendix

Chapter Ten

This chapter is based on information given by the Goldsworthys, the Brewsters, and Norman Hallock.

Sam had told Giny he wanted to be cremated at his death and have his ashes spread over the Sanctuary of Wegimind. According to the Brewsters, Sam made it clear that Giny was not to do this unless she felt comfortable with the idea.

Norman Brewster, who is a local pilot, took his plane Beaver up one day and flew over the region of Four Mile Lake.

The ground fog was so thick that Norm could not see the desired spot. He had just about decided he'd have to come up another day, when the turbulence from the plane parted the fog, and a brilliant shaft of sunlight spotlighted the Sanctuary island which lay directly below.

Norm Brewster released the ashes, which settled quietly over the lake and woodlands so dear to the heart of Sam Campbell.

A small funeral was held in Chicago. According to Norman Hallock, who attended by invitation, thirteen relatives and close friends gathered to remember the wonderful life and work of Sam Campbell.

The testimonial dinner which had been planned for July 29 of 1962 in Three Lakes was held instead as a memorial service for Sam Campbell. The transcript of Sig Olson's remarks at this service were obtained from Walt Goldsworthy and are printed below without change, by permission of Sig Olson's wife Elizabeth Olson of Ely, Minnesota.

Remarks by Mr. Sigurd Olson
At Memorial Service for Sam Campbell
July 29, 1962

It is a great honor for me to be here this evening to be with the friends of Sam Campbell. I am honored to be considered a friend of Sam Campbell, as I know all of you feel too.

This afternoon Mrs. Olson and I spent several hours with Ida and Roy Cunningham at their beautiful home overlooking the lake near town, and with Giny, Sam's wife. While we were there Sam was very close to us. We were talking about the Memorial Service to be held this evening and none of us were sad. Giny, in talking about Sam often remarked how Sam preferred laughter to tears. I know he would have been overjoyed to hear Ernest Swift read the bear story. I can see his eyes twinkling and catching the twinkle in your eyes and all of you laughing together.

This is a joyous occasion and I never think of Sam without thinking of joy. My memory of Sam goes back some thirty years when he first came to the Quetico Superior country to take a canoe trip. I remember vividly the very moment I met him, because from Sam exuded a rare dynamic sort of joy in living—a joy that permeated the atmosphere all around him and affected those with whom he came in contact. It wasn't long before we were all laughing and glad we were alive. Sam had a gladness in living which was rare and unique, and the infectiousness of his gladness was evident wherever he went and whatever he did.

Chapter Ten

I remember the first canoe trip we took together—Sam and his guitar. Portages were always fun; they were adventures. When the winds blew against us, that was fun too. I suddenly realized that when Sam was along everything was fun, and one rainy night we sat in the open door of our tent with a fire in front, and he played his famous guitar and we sang songs. We sang half the night through, though we were wet and somewhat cold and should have been miserable, but we forgot our misery.

I remember at the end of canoe trips and also at the beginning, in those early days, there was a boarding house in the town of Winton where we used to start out, and this boarding house was run lumberjack style by a Finnish woman. Going there was another adventure. I remember how Sam's eyes popped when he took his first look at that table. There was a bunch of lumberjacks there and in the center of the table there was a fifteen pound ham with a bowie knife stuck in the middle and at the other end was a fifteen pound roast beef with another bowie knife in it, pitchers of coffee, milk, tea, deserts, potatoes, vegetables, jam, berries. All that the hostess owned was on that table and the orders were to eat what you could. Sam took one look at that ham and looked at me and then looked at his protege Bobby North, who was with him, and he said, "Bobby, how many pounds do you want?" Bobby said, "Saw it in half!"

Pleasant memories! Memories of joy, memories of gladness, memories of laughter and whenever I think of Sam, it will always be that way.

After I got to know Sam better, I discovered there was something far deeper than just fun and just joy, something that had a basic philosophy, something that indicated a man who had probed the mysteries of life far more deeply than most. Time and again this evening people have mentioned Sam's love: Sam's love of the wilds, Sam's love of animals, Sam's love of people. They might have mentioned too the joy Sam had in seeing his love reciprocated, in knowing that people loved him, that animals loved him, that the very earth loved him. He moved in an aura of love and understanding.

I think Sam would have embraced these words from a sixteenth century monk who gave this advice to his followers. The monk said, "Love all the earth, love every living thing, love every blade of grass, every ray of God's light. If you love enough, you will love all mankind. If you love enough you may become aware of the divine mystery." Sam probably knew what the monk had said, but I am sure whether he knew it or not, that same identical philosophy permeated his whole life and was the mainspring in all he did.

Another facet of Sam's character, and I merely want to touch on two or three of them, very probably was his feeling and consciousness of beauty. The world was a beautiful place to Sam: the lights of the morning and the evening, the sunlight on leaves, moonlight on leaves, the sound of loons calling on the open lakes, bird songs everywhere. Beauty was around him. Like the Navajo he might have said, "Beauty is above me, beauty is around me, I walk in beauty." And I am sure Sam was motivated by what another philosopher said, that the contemplation of beauty century after century is what kept man from the realization of his baser greeds.

I am sure when Sam took his beautiful movies, when he tried to portray to the people of America what a beautiful land this is, that he felt instinctively if he could portray beauty so that people would grasp the beauty of the earth that they would be better. He would inspire them to seek a better life, to think better thoughts and be better people. Beauty and love were part of Sam's life.

One more facet of many, but one I think is important is Sam's awareness, Sam's aliveness, Sam's consciousness of things around him. I am sure he understood the meaning of the Biblical lines, "They have ears but they hear not, eyes but they see not." I know he thought if he could inculcate awareness and understanding and appreciation of the out-of-doors in the millions of people whom he contacted, then he had performed a great service.

In his approach to conservation, Sam had no time to get into the battles that are going on all over the nation, feeling that he could contribute far more by increasing appreciation and understanding among people by using the talents he had—that he could do far more in that way than in any other way. When you think of the tours he and his wife Giny have run off so magnificently, of his radio programs and T.V. appearances; the countless ways in which he has contacted the public, a public who they say conservatively probably runs to nine or ten million people—nine or ten million infecting ten or twenty million more people, no one knows how far his influence has gone. No one knows how far his ideas have permeated, for an idea is like a pebble thrown on the lake and you see the ripples go out toward shore. They finally touch the shore, but no one knows where the vibrations end. And so with the nine or ten millions of people which Sam has surely contacted, nobody knows the tremendous national and internations impact his message has made.

And so, we have come here tonight to do honor to this man, a man who has left us a heritage of joyousness and understanding, of beauty and peace and love and appreciation of the earth and its wildness, its wilderness and its creatures which will never be forgotten. We will always cherish his memory. Three Lakes will always be proud, the nation will always be proud and so in honoring Sam Campbell tonight we honor ourselves and all of us I know are better for having known him.

Giny Campbell remarried in 1970. She and her husband Harold "Hal" E. Kerry moved to a "quiet place in the mountains of Arizona" on the edge of Coconino National Forest. She wrote to Judy Hanson, "We have fun with the birds and animals and keep them well fed!"

Giny passed away in 1982.

Miscellany

Notes on Sam Campbell's Surviving Family

According to Jean Brewster, Sam's brother Don married a lady named "Elsie." Don and Elsie owned the mainland cabin after Sam married and moved to the island. Elsie had two children. The family lived in Boulder, Colorado, and then Texas, where Don passed away some time after Sam's death.

Not much is known about Sam's sister Lucile (Lucille?). According to Three Lakes resident Violet Olkowski, Lucile was living in Florida when Giny Campbell passed away in 1984. Jean Brewster recalls Sam mentioning that Lucile was involved with Irene Castle's work for animal shelters in Chicago.

Identities of Some Characters in Sam Campbell's Books

Most of the characters in Sam Campbell's books were based on real life personalities. He incorporated many of the young people which visited the Sanctuary into his books. Here are the identities of a few.

Character	True Name	Source
Bobby North	Bobby Kostka	Jean Brewster
Duke	Ray Kratz(of Chicago)	"
Ada	Ida Cunningham	"
Ray	Roy Cunningham	"
June	Jean & Beth Cunningham	"
Carol	Phoebe Obermayer and Joanne East (Sam's goddaughter), and others	Giny Campbell, in a letter to JudyHanson

Hi-Bub was "based on a youngster who lived part time in Wisconsin, has moved away from (Three Lakes), married and has a family" according to a July 10, 1975 letter from Giny to Judy Hanson.

Excerpts from Letters

The following excerpts are from correspondence between Giny (Kerry) and Judy Hanson:

```
July 10, 1975
Pinewood Resort
Munds Park, AZ 86001
```

...Sam and I conducted the Sam Campbell Tours from 1948 until his passing in 1962-one private train tour each year. Later, some of the tours were Cruises on luxury ships. We had groups ranging from 190 members as the top figure, down to 128 in the group. After Sam's passing I operated the Sam Campbell Tours (with the help of a large tour organization operating out of Chicago) until 1967...These were called "Nature Lovers" tours, and Sam gave lectures enroute covering the areas we were to visit. Sam used to be the official lecturer for the Chicago and Northwestern Railway, and it was through this contact that the tours started...The first tours were all in the U. S. Later we took folks to Alaska, Hawaii, the South Seas, and to the Baltic Sea area. Later my tours were all to European countries...My groups to Europe were smaller—usually around 30 people...

(signed)
Giny Kerry

July 10, 1975
Pinewood Resort
Munds Park, AZ 86001

Dear Mrs. Hanson:

...Thank you for your loving remarks about my dear Sam and his writings. Yes, we did work very closely together! We had a truly precious companionship and I am so grateful for it. I even enjoyed the canoe trips into the wilderness, though I had been quite a city girl before our marriage...

As to the movie films used with Sam's lectures, these could be of no use to anyone but Sam. These were not sound pictures for Sam was primarily a lecturer and the movies simply illustrated his talks. Some of these wore out and were discarded, other became obsolete...The all animal scenes taken at our Wisconsin home I have kept just for my own personal use. Some of these have become worn and torn and cannot be shown publicly...

A few years after Sam's passing in April 1962, I sold most of our mainland forest holdings to the U. S. Forestry Department. Then about six years ago I sold the island

and a small parcel of land on the mainland to private owners...

Sig's article in the "American Forests" was a beautiful tribute (to Sam). Also—I well remember the fine article of Bill Kay in the C. S. Monitor back in 1948. Everyone did so love and admire Sam, and he dearly loved people. Through his lectures and books he hoped to inspire in people (particularly youngsters) the love of nature and its interesting creatures...

With best wishes,

(signed)
Virginia M. Kerry
(Mrs. Harold E. Kerry)

July 28, 1975
Pinewood Resort
Munds Park, AZ 86001

Dear Mrs. Hanson:

...Yes, the animal characters such as Inky, Salt and Pepper, Eeny, Meeny, Miney, Mo and Still-Mo, Loony Coon, Cheer, etc. including all the baby animals included in *How's Inky* were real and much loved friends of the Campbells. Ancient and Klondike were based upon men Sam had known years ago, and the stories he tells were experiences shared with him by these two characters. The incidents in Sam's books occurred during his life, but they were not always given in the order in which they occurred...

Notes on Sam Campbell's Surviving Family

Sam was a fine specimen of an outdoor man—though he was short! He used to say jokingly he was about the height of a boy scout. He was tall and "big" from the waist up, but short in the legs. He was very broad shouldered and had a 45" chest. He looked as though he could well carry a canoe and a packsack over long trails in the canoe country—and he did! He did wear breeches, Pendleton shirts and suede jackets at all times. (Of course lighter weight shirts in the hot weather.) We even went to Orchestra Hall to symphony concerts, to the Opera etc., Sam wearing such an outfit and very comfortable doing it...And just as a little secret, he wore such clothes when we were married at an outdoor wedding in his sister's garden. I didn't mind a bit, not even his high leather boots. He wore these clothes whether lecturing to schools, women's clubs, men's clubs, or lectures at the various fine Clubs in Chicago, Milwaukee, etc...

Sam at one time taught music: banjo, guitar and the mandolin at his own Studio on Michigan Avenue in Chicago. At one time also he was in the Real Estate business, having an office in downtown Chicago...

Indeed I do agree that his message and philosophy are as equally timely today as when he gave them...I have often thought how happy he would be to see the awareness of people now to the ecology of our world. But he would be very sad to see how far those problems have gone since he left us. He did in a way foresee these things coming, though he did not live to experience them...

You are very perceptive...He told me that at first he did a bit of "crusading" but felt it did not accomplish much. So he lectured to arouse youngsters and adults to LOVE God's universe and her creatures, and thus want to protect them...

Most sincerely,

Giny

The following is from a letter Phoebe Obermayer wrote to Judy Hanson:

August 25, 1975

Dear Judy:

...To begin with, probably the uppermost thoughts that would pertain to Sam, in my mind, would be that he was the gentlest of men, and possessed a limitless ability to love and understand his fellow man and all living things everywhere. There will never be another Sam. His eyes, his smile, his touch and his voice all exuded a magnificent tenderness, but coupled with a deep strength too. When his eyes would meet yours, you would KNOW that he was searching for, and succeeding in, understanding what you were saying and why—and that he cared. His voice had a special quality and his manner of speech was all his own. The smile was utter sincerity and when he expressed interest in what you were saying, you would have a feeling it was intensely genuine. His thought was the deepest I have ever known. And always there was his matchless sense of humor...

When Sam would start to address an audience who had come for his films and lecture, as he did so many thousands of times, he would express appreciation for their coming, and lead into a thrilling, inspiring, and heart-warming narrative about the world in general, people everywhere, God's ideas and plans for each of us, and the hows and whys of the guidance from God available to all of us...It is difficult if not impossible to describe the inspiration that Sam brought to his listeners. It was so unique and so sincere, no one could come away without being moved...

My own friendship with Sam began before my teens, when my parents brought me to one of his lectures. I have always had a great love for animals, and even at that age, was delighted beyond description to hear Sam talk of HIS love for animals and all living things. I somehow found the courage to introduce myself to him after the lecture. Not long after that, I began corresponding with Giny and Sam and this soon led to the first of my many cherished visits to the Sanctuary of Wegimind.

I have countless treasured memories of those years. Many hours were spent in warm give-and-take conversations, discussing ideas on an unlimited number of things, with Sam and Giny's thoughts always an inspiration. One very vivid aspect of my memory of

Sam was his incomparable sense of humor. It was irrepressible and a twinkle in the eye was ever present. There was much good fun and laughter in his company...Sam's humor was, of course, a beautiful one, never at anyone's expense. His capacity for fun was equaled by Giny's.

The name "Giny" is a dear one. Here is an angel, with a capacity unexcelled for love, devotion, unselfishness, kindness and thoughtfulness. She is completely and utterly devoted to God, His creation and all in it, and is dearly cherished by all who know her.

At the Sanctuary, we enjoyed many hikes in the lovely north woods country. Autumn was a particular favorite of mine, with the woods breathtaking in their shade of red and gold. Vanishing Lake was always a thrill, and the sight of deer was always a big event. What fun it was to be greeted at the pier by Salt and Pepper! Among the most beautiful of my memories are those of our campfire circle, Sam and Giny leading us in song; and the breathtaking canoe rides, Giny paddling in front and Sam in back, late in the evening when the water was still as glass, and we could hear distant calls across the lake, and would stare unbelievingly at the Northern Lights. No one would speak to break this incredible spell...

Judy, I have included much in my letter of a personal nature, but somehow it was impossible to write of Sam otherwise...

Notes on Sam Campbell's Surviving Family

Cordially,
(signed Phoebe)

From a letter Ida Cunningham wrote to Judy Hanson:

July 7, 1975
Three Lakes, WI

Dear Mrs. Hanson:

...I never knew the character called "Hi-Bub", but I am sure Giny may give you some information about him. The characters in Sam's books were a compilation of various individuals, "fiction based upon fact" as he characterized his writing, and it would be difficult to identify any one character. My husband, now deceased, and I together with our children, and later Giny, that many of our experiences became theirs in the writings, as we were year round residents of the area and carried on his work, like feeding bears and raccoons when he was on lecture tours, etc... I do know that the film footage that Sam used in lectures is stored at a friend's home in the Chicago area. There is a Forest Plaque erected by the U. S. Forest Service in an area including Vanishing Lake that Giny presented to the Forest Service after Sam's passing...

Sincerely,

(signed)
Ida M. Cunningham

SAM CAMPBELL Philosopher Of The Forest

The following is from a letter written by Sigurd F. Olson:

July 16, 1975
Ely, MN

Dear Judy Hanson:

...I made several short canoe trips with (Sam) and he visited a number of times at our home. Each trip was sheer delight, for his pixiish sense of humor, of seeing something to smile or laugh at wherever he went, made it impossible to be anything but happy. When with him we all became children again. One of the most vivid memories was his sitting by the fire playing his guitar. The magic he brought out of that instrument affected us all and when we sang together life was complete. One place where we were camped beside a little place called "Singing Rapids" between Burke and Sunday Lakes in the Quetico, it seemed as though he caught the music of the water in his playing, simulated the sound of its singing.

No bad weather, wind, or plagues of flies and mosquitoes ever bothered him. He could laugh at it all. A true woodsman, a true son of the North. He epitomized what he dreamed and wrote about. A force for good in environmental awareness, he was one of the first to preach the gospel to millions at a time when ecology and environment were almost unknown. He laid the groundwork and his influence goes on. Now the children are grown but they carry in their hearts and in their lives the message Sam left with them.

Sincerely,
(Signed)
Sigurd F. Olson

Notes on Sam Campbell's Surviving Family

A letter from Dorothy J. Hoelter to the author:

July 2, 1991
La Mesa, CA

Dear Ms. Henson:

...I have fond memories of visiting Sam Campbell's home when I was in my teens. Several young women with their mothers, and Jean Brewster and her sister Beth and their mother Ida Cunningham, shared some very nice experiences at his home in Three Lakes. We enjoyed the walks each day on the trails and saw a great deal. Many animals befriended us, and we felt close to them.

Each evening we would go for a ride and see deer in the meadows. You can imagine what a treat this was for young women raised in a busy city...On one evening (Sam) was wakened and had to shoo the bats out of the bedroom and ...then another evening...a little mouse ran across the floor and all of us screamed.

He made us sit down and be still and watch that little mouse perform all of its antics. This was very thrilling for us, and I am sure it took away a lot of fear we had at that time...

I remember the wonderful fireplace Sam had. And the good barbecues. He often cooked steaks in the fireplace. I was acting as a secretary for Sam and remember the first letter he received from Ginny (sic). She had heard him lecture on the North Woods and wrote to thank him: their romance continued from that point. She was so right for him, and they enjoyed many happy years together visiting many parks and wilderness areas together. She enjoyed nature and animals as much as Sam did. I know she was very helpful and supportive in Sam's work...

Sincerely,

(signed)
Dorothy J. Hoelter

The Kieckhefer family now owns the old Campbell home in Barrington, IL. Robert Kieckhefer wrote to the author:

May 9, 1991
LaFayette, CA

Dear Ms. Henson:

Sam Campbell, my father said, could get more mileage out of a chipmunk than any man alive...

I was 4 years old when I moved next door to Ginny (sic) and Sam in Barrinton. We lived on 5-acre lots that had been carved out of a large dairy farm. The woods included majestic white oaks and burr oaks that stood above grasslands in the days the cows grazed the property, and a potpourri of smaller brush that took root after the cows had left, perhaps five years before we arrived. The woods were thick enough that we couldn't see any of our neighbors' houses during the summer...

My (extended) family owned a cabin on Butternut Lake, only a few miles from the Campbells' Three Lakes cabin...Their cabin was a wonderfully secluded place, surrounded by towering pines. But of most interest to me were the squirrels, who Sam had tamed. I (fed) them corn and sunflower seeds. One would even run up my leg to take food from my hand. So this was how he learned enough about animals to write about them!

Sincerely yours,

(signed)

R. M. Kieckhefer

Ralph Leatzow gave the author a copy of the following letter from Ernest Wise to Sam Campbell:

January 17, 1949
Greenville, IL

Dear Sam Campbell:

I am mailing to you—enclosed—three deeds to the nearest 10 acres on the Lonestone Trail, because you now own that land. I think it is good to preserve such deeds, as occasionally the courthouse records are destroyed. That happened in Greenville in 1880 when the courthouse burned and the record vault did not hold up.

This man Bierbrauer was living as a hermit on Brown's point, the only person who lived on Four Mile Lake. He suggested we come out with our tents and camp awhile. Then he took me over the land and suggested I buy it. So I hired a man with a one horse wagon and we made the trip to Eagle River and purchased it from the homesteader. Bierbrauer had his garden on the point this side of the Lonestone Trail, and as he did such good work for us for about a year, we made him a present of this land. As soon as he received the deed, he sold to the Russells, moved down to Planting Ground Lake and returned to his drunken ways which soon cost him his life.

Four years later the Russells sold it to me and later I sold the entire Lot No. Two (2) to the Sheriff from Ashland, Wisconsin.

Mrs. Wise has been reading to me your column in the Three Lakes News—"I've Been Thinking." <u>We certainly enjoyed every bit of it!</u>

Sincere good wishes to you and Mrs. Campbell from Mrs. Wise and (signed Ernest E. Wise).

Jean Brewster wrote the following regarding the story of "Ludy" the loon which Sam told in *Too Much Salt and Pepper*.

November 14, 1989
Three Lakes, WI

Dear Shandelle:

...You asked about Ludy the loon. Yes, he was a big part of our life and much loved for one whole winter. My brother was walking along a lake near our home and saw the bird helpless out on the ice. They cannot take off to fly, of course, except from open water, because of the placement of their feet...unlike geese and some ducks who land in fields, etc. Apparently the bird had come down onto the ice, thinking it was open water, and so was helpless.

Notes on Sam Campbell's Surviving Family

Howard (at great risk, as he was later reminded by my parents) crawled out onto that new ice, wrapped his jacket around the bird and brought him home. It was quite an experience, learning what to feed him, etc. Eventually he settled in, living in a tub under the kitchen table, and joining the family circle on winter evenings around the floor register...we did have him until spring, and then it was a day to weep (but still be grateful for the experience) when he sat on the porch, looking up at the spring sky, gave a long haunting call, then went quietly to sleep forever.

Best from all here,
(signed, Jean Brewster)

SAM CAMPBELL Philosopher Of The Forest

Notes on Sam Campbell's Surviving Family

SAM CAMPBELL TOURS

Home and Office
220 OAK KNOLL ROAD
BARRINGTON, ILLINOIS

July 7, 1961

books by Sam Campbell:

How's Inky
Too Much Salt and Pepper
Eeny Meeny Miney Mo & Still-Mo
A Tippy Canoe and Canada Too
On Wings of Cheer
Moose Country
The Seven Secrets of Somewhere Lake
Loony Coon
Fiddlesticks and Freckles
Nature's Messages
Beloved Rascals
Sweet Sue's Adventures

Mr. Walt Goldsworthy
Three Lakes, Wisconsin

Dear Walt,

        We just returned from Europe yesterday. Your letter was waiting patiently for us, and waiting a long time.

        Now we are clearing up some details of the European Cruise, and then we will come north. HURRAY! After visiting 8 foreign countries, and 14 ports, we come back convinced more than ever that Three Lakes is the greatest spot on earth.

        Now Walt, it is mighty nice of you to come up with that idea of a testimonial banquet for me. Surely I could not refuse such a pleasureable affair, particularly as it involves friends and country I love so deeply.

        However, I am late arriving in the north (expect to be there between July 15th and 20th, xto stay until Oct. 1st). Perhaps there is not time to develop the event properly. Also, remember Walt, not everyone has approved of me in that community -- perhaps some would resent this honor being shown me. You will know the answer to the points I have brought up.

        Will see you fairly soon. Best to you and your family.

Sincerely

Sam

"THE PHILOSOPHER OF THE FOREST"

SAM CAMPBELL Philosopher Of The Forest

S A M   C A M P B E L L
The Sam Campbell Tours—Nature Lectures
220 OAK KNOLL ROAD
BARRINGTON, ILL.

January 31, 1961

books by Sam Campbell:

How's Inky
Too Much Salt and Pepper
Eeny Meeny Miney Mo & Still-Me
A Tippy Canoe and Canada Too
On Wings of Cheer
Moose Country
The Seven Secrets of Somewhere Lake
Loony Coon
Fiddlesticks and Freckles
Nature's Messages
Beloved Rascals

Dear Walt Goldsworthy,

    Due to my own busy program, I just received the Souvenir Program of the Three Lakes Winter Carnival, which you kindly sent to me.

    It is splendidly done, Walt, and I wish you would extend my congratulations to all who had a part in it. I would feel better had I known of the booklet early enough to subscribe to it.

    It isn't easy to stir up the energy and ambition to carry out such projects. It is proverbial that the work generally gravitates to just a few. There is no reason to gripe about this. The world has always been that way. Folks like yourself, Ed Boehm, Ed Kane and others, are born with the stamina and enthusiasm to work hard, and I guess you'll always have to do it. Your reward for the most part must be in "mission accomplished." Gratitude from others is insufficient or totally lacking. I think this lack is not so much in a failure to feel gratitude, as in failure to express it. Lest I be guilty of this very thing, let me here thank you and the others for what you have done.

    To carry this thought a little farther, I want to express appreciation for your articles in the Three Lakes News. Your writing is crisp, lively, and interesting. You handle an amazing amount of subject matter in a scholarly way. That kind of writing is not easy to do. Thank you for your continuous contribution.

Most cordially,

Sam

Am enclosing the folder of our next Cruise. To our great surprise we are sold out, with 120 people on the list.

" T H E   P H I L O S O P H E R   O F   T H E   F O R E S T "

Notes on Sam Campbell's Surviving Family

SAM CAMPBELL
The Sam Campbell Tours—Nature Lectures
220 OAK KNOLL ROAD
BARRINGTON, ILL.

February 27, 1962

Dear WALT and Sig,

Darned if it doesn't look like that there now Testimonial Dinner is gonna be a fact! With all the things you say, Walt, I am beginning to feel (a little) like John Glen.

Well, it's no use to pretend it doesn't please me. I love my friends, deeply, sincerely, and I want them to love me. That last sentence really is my formula for happiness.

Now as to the date -- really any one is all right with me. Still, I have my druthers. Wednesday I like the least. I suggest Thursday, July 26 as first choice, and Saturday, July 28 as second.

Walt, I suggest no parade. I would be embarrassed at such a display. I am so conscious of my own unworthiness, I would prefer that we make this a display of friendship, rather than honors. Really I have done so little in the world. But if what I have done has benefitted my beloved Three Lakes, I am grateful.

Sig -- if it works out for you to be present at this event (I hope, I hope), Giny and I would like you and Elizabeth to be our guests on the island for as long as you can stay. I promise to cook a steak you'll never forget -- for one reason or another.

Sorry Dr. Harvey will be away. No one else among the summer people for MC comes to mind immediately, so I'll give this angle some more thought. How about our radio announcer from Rhinelander? He is experienced, and quite professional in attitude.

No doubt Sig will write now on the matter of date -- and his decision is my decision.

Best to you both,

Sam

"THE PHILOSOPHER OF THE FOREST"

SAM CAMPBELL Philosopher Of The Forest

SAM CAMPBELL
The Sam Campbell Touch Nature Lectures
320 OAK KNOLL ROAD
BARRINGTON, ILL.

April 4, 1952

books by Sam Campbell:
Flicky Inky
Too Much Salt and Pepper
Eeny Meeny Miney Moe &
  Still-Mo
A Tippy Canoe and Canada
  Too
On Wings of Cheer
Moose Country
The Seven Secrets of
  Somewhere Lake
Loony Coon
Fiddlesticks and Freckles
Beloved Rascals
Sweet Sue's Adventures

Dear Walt

Herewith is the biographical outline. I just let myself wander all over the typewriter in doing it, figuring that you will re-write the material to fit the various publications.

No, Walt, I am not a member of the Izaak Walton League, so I presume that is out. I have been an honorary member of branches at various times, but presume this does not count. Don't know just why I haven't become a member, but I haven't.

It was grand to have you and Ed drop in. Giny and I are still talking about it. Hope you can do it again.

I shall leave here April 29th, and return here June 2nd. Should be north by June 15th.

Best to you

Sam

"THE PHILOSOPHER OF THE FOREST"

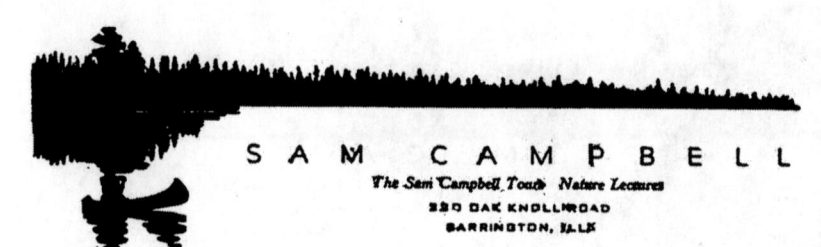

Notes on Sam Campbell's Surviving Family

SAM CAMPBELL TOURS

March 14, 1964

Home and Office
220 OAK KNOLL ROAD
BARRINGTON, ILLINOIS
DUnkirk 1-1898

books by Sam Campbell:

How's Inky
Too Much Salt and Pepper
Eeny Meeny Miney Mo & Still-Mo
A Tippy Canoe and Canada Too
On Wings of Cheer
Moose Country
The Seven Secrets of Somewhere Lake
Loony Coon
Fiddlesticks and Freckles
Nature's Messages
Beloved Rascals
Sweet Sue's Adventures
Calamity Jane

Dear Walt:

What an ambitious boy you are! — another fine column under "Walt's Journal." The readers of the Rhinelander Daily News have many happy hours in store for them enjoying your fine inspirational writing. Congratulations!

It was so good to see your reference once more to my dear one. I too think of Sam when I see Capella sparkling in the heavens. That star was sort of a personal friend of Sam's. Thank you for keeping Sammie alive in your heart Walt.

By this time you have my little note written a few days ago. No doubt our envelopes passed each other in the mails.

Best to you and your lovely family always!

Most sincerely,

Mrs. Sam Campbell

131

SAM CAMPBELL Philosopher Of The Forest

work the Forestry Department is doing.

SAM CAMPBELL TOURS

August 5, 1964

Home and Office
Mrs. Sam Campbell
3550 Lake Shore Drive
Chicago, Illinois 60657

Mr. Walter Goldsworthy
Three Lakes,
Wisconsin

books by Sam Campbell:

How's Inky
Too Much Salt and Pepper
Eeny Meeny Miney Mo & Still-Mo
A Tippy Canoe and Canada Too
On Wings of Cheer
Moose Country
The Seven Secrets of Somewhere Lake
Loony Coon
Fiddlesticks and Freckles
Nature's Messages
Beloved Rascals
Sweet Sue's Adventures
Calamity Jane

Dear Walt:

    Greetings from my apartment in Chicago! Shortly after our wonderful Dedication Services at the Memorial Service, I left for the city and have been in quite a mad whirl since getting here. Otherwise, I would have written you sooner.

    It is my sincere desire to thank you from the bottom of my heart for your heroic efforts in behalf of the Sam Campbell Memorial, Walt! It takes someone like your fine self, with love for what he is doing, and the necessary drive - to accomplish these things. Everything went off so nicely, and you and Doris did so much to make it the fine occasion it was. Thank you both so much.

    Everyone who spoke at the Dedication did so well and I believe we had a very nice crowd there considering the short time we had to publicize it. It was another red-letter day for me to remember as long as I live. As Cy said, "How do we know that Sam wasn't aware of that whole wonderful tribute to him?" These are not Cy's own words, but the idea is there. God bless you all.

    I like your words about a trail through the 140 acres, around Vanishing Lake, etc. to the marker. Let's talk more about this? Will see you the last week in September, Walt.

    When I come home, will take time to contact the A.C. Rehberger Co. in Chicago about the making of a suitable bronze plaque. Perhaps we will have to shorten the number of words on the plaque Walt, to bring it within reason as to price. Am sure something can be worked out. More on this when I see you.

Most gratefully,

Mrs. Sam Campbell

Notes on Sam Campbell's Surviving Family

The old Campbell campsite on the east shore of Four mile Lake.

Top to Bottom:

Mr. Sloan, "Dad" Campbell and Roy Cunningham working on Vanishing Lake Trail; Ida Cunningham on Vanishing Lake Trail; "Dad" Campbell, Roy Campbell, and Mr. Slon on Vanishing Lake Trail.

Notes on Sam Campbell's Surviving Family

Top to Bottom:

Roy Cunningham, Mr. Sloan, Ida Cunningham, "Dad" Campbell, and Sam Campbell on the trail to Vanishing Lake;

A campfire supper with Gene Gunderson, "Dad" Campbell, Nina Gunderson, Art Merigold, Beda Wagers. Ralph Wagers, Sam Campbell, and Ida Cunningham.

135

Trail Markers:

Vanishing Lake Trail "The drying of a single tear has more of honest fame than shedding seas of gore." —Bryon

Friendship Trail "Nina Gunderson"

Notes on Sam Campbell's Surviving Family

Campbell Island on Four Mile Lake in the Sanctuary of Wegimind.

Sam's canoe yoke.

The old Three Lakes train station.

Sam Campbell

Notes on Sam Campbell's Surviving Family

The Sanctuary of Wegimind

The Finding of Vanishing Lake

Ebony Mansions

Naturalness

Frozen Memories

"Sanctuary Letters"
Five early essays bound in velvet.

SAM CAMPBELL Philosopher Of The Forest

Counterclockwise from top:
Sam Campbell addressing Boy Scouts:
Ida and Roy Cunningham:
SamCampbell in 1937.

Notes on Sam Campbell's Surviving Family

These pictures are from a photo album entitled "Memories of a Wonderful Week at the Sanctuary," by Giny Adams.

Counterclockwise from top left:

"A Lovely Entrance;" "The Congregation;" "Just Giny Enjoying the Island."

The
island
cabin

Notes on Sam Campbell's Surviving Family

The island
workroom
and boathouse.

SAM CAMPBELL Philosopher Of The Forest

The cabin livingroom.

Notes on Sam Campbell's Surviving Family

The cabin kitchen and bunkroom.

Counterclockwise from top left:

Jean Cunningham, Giny Campbell, and Beth Cunningham; Norm Brewster; Roy and Ida Cunningham.

Notes on Sam Campbell's Surviving Family

Sam with his animal friends.

Sam with animal friends.

Notes on Sam Campbell's Surviving Family

Counterclockwise from top:
Campbells' and Cunninghams' camp on Sarah Lake in canoe country; Sam Campbell and Roy Cunningham bring in supper on Sarah Lake; Sam Campbell in canoe country.

Sam and Giny.

Notes on Sam Campbell's Surviving Family

Sam and Giny
on lecture tour

151

SAM CAMPBELL Philosopher Of The Forest

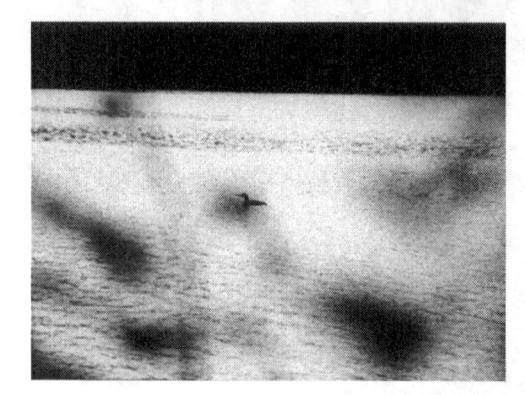

A loon on Four Mile Lake.

Giny Campbell

Notes on Sam Campbell's Surviving Family

Sigurd Olson presents memorial plaque to Giny Campbell.

George Richards, Walt Goldsworthy, M. S. Harvey, and Sam Campbell. Plaque awarded to Walt Goldsworthy for conservation work.

SAM CAMPBELL Philosopher Of The Forest

The old church in Eagle River (now an antique shop).

The new church in Eagle River.

Walt Goldsworthy and the Three Lakes Museum's Sam Campbell Collection.

The author on the Sam Campbell Trail.

Sam Campbell Road.

SAM CAMPBELL Philosopher Of The Forest

Bibliography

Benyus, Janine M. *Northwoods Wildlife*.
A Watcher's Guide to Habitats. Minocqua, Wisconsin, Lake States Interpretive Association, 1989.

Campbell, Sam. *Beloved Rascals*.
Indianapolis and New York, The Bobbs-Merrill Company, Inc., 1957.

___*Calamity Jane*. The Wise Old Raccoon.
Indianapolis and New York, The Bobbs-Merrill Company, Inc., 1962.

___*The Conquest of Grief*. Sam Campbell, 1933.

___*Eeny, Meeny, Miney, Mo—and Still-Mo*.
Indianapolis and New York, The Bobbs-Merrill Company, Inc., 1945.

___*Fiddlesticks and Freckles*.
Indianapolis and New York, The Bobbs-Merrill Company, Inc., 1955.

___*How's Inky?*
Indianapolis and New York, The Bobbs-Merrill Company, Inc., 1943.

___*Loony Coon*.
Indianapolis and New York, The Bobbs-Merrill Company, Inc., 1954.

___*Moose Country*.
Indianapolis and New York, The Bobbs-Merrill Company, Inc., 1950.

___*Nature's Messages*.
New York and Chicago and San Francisco, Rand McNally & Company, 1952.

___*On Wings of Cheer*.
Indianapolis and New York, The Bobbs-Merrill Company, Inc., 1948.

___*The Seven Secrets of Somewhere Lake*.
Indianapolis and New York, The Bobbs-Merrill Company, Inc., 1952.

___*Sweet Sue's Adventures*.
Indianapolis and New York, The Bobbs-Merrill Company, Inc., 1959.

___*A Tippy Canoe and Canada Too*.
Indianaoplis and New York, The Bobbs-Merrill Company, Inc., 1946.

___*Too Much Salt and Pepper*.
Indianapolis and New York, The Bobbs-Merrill Company, Inc., 1944.

___*Woodland Portraits*. Milwaukee, Ideals Press, 1974.

Eifert, Virginia S. *Land of the Snowshoe Hare.*
New York, Dodd, Mead & Company, 1960.

Goldsworthy, Walter. *Wilderness Reflections.*
Milwaukee, Ideals Press, 1977.

Nute, Grace Lee. *The Voyageur's Highway.*
St. Paul, Minnesota Historical Society, 1941, 1969.

Olson, Sigurd F. *The Singing Wilderness.*
New York, Alfred A. Knopf, Inc., 1956.

The Pine, the Plow and the Pioneer. Vol. I
and II. Three Lakes, Wisconsin, Three Lakes
Historical Society, Inc., 1984 and 1986.

Portrait and Bibliographical Record of Iroquois County, Illinois. Chicago, Lake City Publishing Company, 1893.

Who's Who in America. Vol. 32. Chicago, A. N. Marquis & Company, 1962–1963.

The author explores canoe country in 1993

Shandelle Marie Henson was born in 1964 in Cleveland, Tennessee and was raised on a farm in the Tennessee hills. She received a Bachelors in Mathematics from Southern College of Seventh-day Adventists, Collegedale, Tennessee (1987); a Masters in Mathematics from Duke University, Durham, North Carolina (1989); and a PhD in Mathematics from the University of Tennessee, Knoxville (1994). She teaches and does research in ecological modeling at the University of Arizona, Tucson. She loves animals, wilderness, mountain running, backpacking, music, and time alone with God in solitude.

We'd love to have you download our catalog of
titles we publish at:

www.TEACHServices.com

or write or email us your thoughts,
reactions, or criticism about this
or any other book we publish at:

TEACH Services, Inc.
254 Donovan Road
Brushton, NY 12916

info@TEACHServices.com

or you may call us at:

518/358-3494